Emergencies at Sea

CHAPMAN'S
Nautical Guides

Emergencies at Sea

by Sid Stapleton
illustrations by Ralph Futrell

HEARST MARINE BOOKS
New York

Library of Congress Catalog Card Number: 90-81985

ISBN: 0-688-09755-3

Printed in Italy
First U.S. Edition
1 2 3 4 5 6 7 8 9 10

Edited by Lucy A. O'Brien
Produced by Smallwood and Stewart Inc.
9 West 19th Street
New York, N.Y. 10011

NOTICE: The author and publisher disclaim responsibility for any adverse
effects or consequences resulting from the suggestions or the use of any of
the preparations or procedures contained herein.

The medical and health procedures contained in this book are based on
research and recommendations of responsible medical sources. But because
each person is unique, the author and publisher urge the reader, when
circumstances permit, to check with a physician before implementing
any of them.

CONTENTS

INTRODUCTION

You're well offshore on a fishing trip when suddenly oily black smoke starts billowing out of your boat's engine room. Do you know what to do—and, equally important, what not to do—to improve your chances that the fire won't completely destroy your vessel, forcing you to abandon it far out at sea?

You're on an overnight run on a black and violent night when your vessel strikes a submerged object and water starts gushing into the hull. You quickly realize that the flood is far greater than your bilge pump can handle. Is there anything you can do to help keep your boat from foundering? If you can't prevent her from sinking, do you know what you need to do—and in what order—to get your crew safely into your life raft and increase your chances of being rescued quickly?

You're out for a pleasant day's sail when one of your foredeck crew takes a nasty fall and strikes his or her head on a deck cleat. The victim is bleeding profusely, is disoriented and pale, and seems about to pass out. Do you know what must be done during that first "golden hour" following a traumatic injury until you can get the victim to professional medical help?

Everything aboard your own vessel is perfectly squared away, but over your radio you hear a Mayday call from a vessel just a mile or so distant. The signal is weak and yours is apparently the only vessel in the vicinity. Simply hearing that call imposes on you a number of legal obligations. Do you know what they are? Do you know what you must do to discharge them?

To provide the answers to these questions and dozens of others that you might have in an emergency situation afloat—and to present them in a concise, one-two-three format that you can use instantly when trouble strikes—is the purpose of this book.

Those of us who love being at sea experience a sense of freedom and independence that landlubbers find difficult to comprehend. But our freedom and independence carry with them a special responsibility to be prepared, not only to handle virtually any emergency that might arise on board our own vessels, but to assist others who might be faced with a potentially life-threatening situation. A hundred miles offshore, or even in the middle of a sizable bay or lake, the fire department is a good deal farther away than just down the block; we can't simply dial 911 and expect an ambulance to come screaming around the corner. If we encounter someone else in trouble we can't just shrug our shoulders and say, "Let the professionals handle it." While we can't be expected to be expert fire fighters or trauma physicians, we should at least be equipped and knowledgeable enough to avoid making any crisis we encounter worse. It is hoped that we shall also be able to take appropriate, well-informed steps to prevent loss of life or serious injury both to those entrusted to us on our vessels and to any others we might one day be called upon to help.

The focus of this book, then, is what to do the instant trouble erupts. It begins with the assumption that you have already outfitted your vessel with appropriate life jackets, a good life raft, the right kind of extinguishers to fight both fuel and electrical fires, and all the other safety gear that should be aboard any well-equipped recreational vessel. It also assumes that you have properly prepared yourself and your crew to handle potential emergencies by taking a comprehensive first-aid course, by thoroughly briefing yourself on the proper operation of all the safety equipment on board, and by conducting periodic crew training in everything from man-overboard to abandon-ship drills.

A word about this book's format. Chapters are arranged alphabetically. At the head of each chapter is a series of steps you should follow in order to deal with the situation being covered. You may be surprised at some of the recommendations. Some may contain information of which you are not aware or which you had never considered. You may, in fact, find that some of them contradict procedures you've long held to be gospel truth.

For these reasons, the meat of each chapter is a discussion of the whys and wherefores behind each of the recommended steps, as well as behind the order in which they are presented. Most of the chapters follow the opening sections with a discussion of more general tips and hints regarding things you might not need to know immediately in order to deal with a specific emergency but might like to have tucked away in the back of your mind.

The recommendations you find here are not based simply on armchair "what if" musings. They are based on the accumulated knowledge gleaned from more than twenty years of cruising and fishing around the world on a wide variety of vessels, both my own and those of other boat owners who have been kind enough to let me tag along. And for every topic, I've extensively interviewed the people who should have the straight stuff: the pilots who fly search-and-rescue aircraft; the people who run the satellite systems that silently scan the earth for us if we get into a jam; the experts in marine fire-fighting; the wizards who design the marine radios, EPIRBs (Emergency Position-Indicating Radio Beacons), life rafts, and parachute flares to which you one day might have to trust your own life and the lives of others.

My hope is that you will read this book from cover to cover before you ever need any of its information, then review it periodically to keep yourself up-to-date. Stow it in a handy location on board, where you can snatch it quickly in an emergency. Under the stress of a situation that places your vessel or the lives of others in danger, it is easy for even the most experienced mariner to forget to do something crucial or to jumble the order of the steps that need to be taken, which can create unnecessary confusion or waste valuable time.

With luck, you will never have an emergency aboard your vessel serious enough to have to use this book in earnest. But forewarned is forearmed. And, if your luck runs a little short some dark and stormy night, and you find a really nasty situation staring you in the face, demanding that you do the right thing right now, I hope you'll find a bit of reassurance in being able to grab this book and know that you are doing what you need to do, in the way you need to do it in order to keep yourself and all those aboard your vessel as safe and healthy as possible.

CHAPTER ONE

ABANDONING SHIP

- Abandon ship only as a last resort.

- Make certain all crew members are warmly dressed and wearing life jackets. In waters below 60° F, crew members should also put on immersion suits.

- Instruct a trained crew member to stand by life raft and prepare to launch it.

- Transmit a Mayday distress call and message.

- Gather abandon-ship bag and other emergency supplies.

- Make certain life raft is tethered to vessel and launch it. In heavy seas, launch to leeward amidships.

- Load crew and emergency supplies into life raft.

- Activate EPIRB and fire one red meteor or parachute flare.

- Keep life raft tethered to main vessel for as long as possible.

- **Abandon ship only as a last resort.**

The act of abandoning ship is a procedure filled with potential hazards and should be undertaken only if your vessel is fully on fire or is in imminent danger of sinking. In many cases, even vessels that have been seriously holed will remain afloat for hours, or even days, due to their natural buoyancy or to air trapped inside their hulls or superstructures.

At the first inkling that a fire or a breach of your hull's integrity may become grave enough to require you to abandon ship, mentally run through the steps the procedure requires and alert your crew that you are considering that extreme course of action. But don't give the actual abandon-ship order until you are certain there is no way you can contain the fire or the hull damage to allow you and your crew to remain on board until help arrives. (The recommended procedures for fighting a fire on board are covered fully on pages 31-44. Recommended procedures for dealing with severe hull damage will be found on pages 75-81.)

- **Make certain all crew members are warmly dressed and wearing life jackets. In waters below 60° F, crew members should also put on immersion suits.**

If the situation aboard your vessel is serious enough for you to consider abandoning ship, you and your crew may already be dressed in warm clothes and wearing life jackets. But if a serious emergency arises suddenly (for example, a fire or severe hull damage resulting from striking a submerged object in the middle of the night), as soon as you even wonder if you might have to abandon ship, put on warm clothes and your own life jacket and order your crew to do likewise. If you have to order your crew into the raft, they could very well wind up in the water, and warm clothing and a life jacket could prove to be, literally, the difference between life and death.

Exposure to hypothermia (extreme loss of body heat) is one of the greatest dangers you and your crew will face in the abandon-ship situation. Long pants, long-sleeved shirts, sweaters, and jackets can help preserve valuable body heat, even if they are soaked.

In offshore situations, all the life jackets aboard your vessel should be Type I and, at a minimum, should be fitted with reflective patches and a whistle. It's even better to also equip each of them with a strobe-type personal rescue light and mini-B or Class S EPIRB.

Immersion suits are cumbersome and expensive, but they are absolute necessities aboard any vessel that ventures into waters 60° F or colder. Without an immersion suit, survival times in waters of that temperature can be less than an hour. Wearing an immersion suit, you are likely to survive up to eight times longer than you would without one.

- **Instruct a trained crew member to stand by life raft and prepare to launch it**

As a part of the routine safety training aboard your vessel, you should have thoroughly familiarized at least one crew member with your life raft and its proper deployment. That crew member should, for instance, know to make sure that the raft is tethered to the main vessel before it is launched. Ideally, you will stow your life raft on deck in its own canister, and it will be equipped with a CO_2 automatic inflation device. If you carry your life raft below decks and/or it must be manually inflated, the crew member should know where it is located, how to inflate it quickly, and to inflate it on deck rather than belowdecks or in the cockpit.

- **Transmit a Mayday distress call and message.**

Transmit the Mayday distress call and message the moment the situation aboard your vessel becomes serious enough for you to decide to abandon ship. If you delay doing so, rising water or fire could disable the batteries that power your radio in a matter of minutes.

The circumstances under which you should transmit either the Pan-Pan urgency call and message or the Mayday distress call and message and the correct procedures for doing so are covered fully on pages 177-190. To briefly recap the procedure for transmitting the Mayday distress call and message:

1. If your marine radio is equipped with a radio-telephone alarm signal, activate it for 30 seconds if possible, but not for more than one minute, before you transmit the distress call and message to attract attention to them and to activate any automatic equipment that might receive them.

2. If within about 20 miles of shore, transmit the Mayday distress call and message first on VHF Channel 16 (156.8 MHz). If offshore more than 20 miles, transmit them first on SSB frequency 2182 kHz.

3. Transmit the Mayday call and distress message using the format in Fig. 1.1.

After transmitting the distress call and message, wait 30 seconds for any vessel receiving it to respond. If there is no response, transmit the distress call and message (preceded by a radiotelephone alarm signal, if possible) a second time over that same channel. If there is still no answer, retransmit the distress call and message—preceded if possible by a radiotelephone alarm signal—on any channel frequently used in the area. Good second choices on VHF would be Channel

FORMAT FOR TRANSMITTING
Mayday DISTRESS CALL AND MESSAGE

Fill this form out for your vessel. Speak SLOWLY—CLEARLY—CALMLY.

1. Activate international radiotelephone alarm signal.

2. "MAYDAY—MAYDAY—MAYDAY."

3. "THIS IS _____ _____, _____."
   (your boat name)   (your boat name)

   _____, _____."
   (your boat name)   (your call sign)

4. "MAYDAY: _____."
   (your boat name)

5. "POSITION IS: _____."
   (your vessel's position in degrees and minutes of latitude NORTH or SOUTH and longitude EAST or WEST; or as distance and bearing [magnetic or true] to well-known navigation landmark)

6. "WE _____."
   (state nature of your emergency)

7. "WE REQUIRE _____."
   (state type of assistance required)

8. "ABOARD ARE _____."
   (give number of adults and children on board and conditions of any injured)

9. "_____ IS A _____-FOOT
   (your boat name)   (length of your boat in feet)

   _____ WITH A _____
   (type: sloop, motor yacht, etc.)   (hull color)

   HULL AND _____ TRIM."
   (color of trim)

10. "I WILL BE LISTENING ON CHANNEL 16/2182."
    (cross out channel or frequency that does not apply)

11. "THIS IS _____, _____."
    (your boat name)   (and call sign)

12. "OVER."

Figure 1.1

22A (157.1 MHz), which is the primary Coast Guard liaison channel, or Channel 72 (156.625 MHz), which at sea is used as an international ship-to-ship channel. Good second choice SSB frequencies would be 2670 kHz, a primary Coast Guard working channel, and ITU Channel 424 (ship's transmit carrier 4134.3 kHz; ship's receive carrier, 4428.7 kHz), which is continuously monitored by the Coast Guard as part of its Contact and Long Range Liaison (CALL) system.

- **Gather abandon-ship bag and other emergency supplies.**

Your abandon-ship bag should be stowed where you can grab it quickly on your way to the life raft. A list of suggested contents for the bag is given in Fig. 1.2. The abandon-ship bag should be fitted with flotation and a 50-foot floating lanyard, which with luck you will have time to attach to your life raft before you leave your vessel. Its most important content will be at least a half-gallon of fresh water per person or a hand-operated reverse osmosis watermaker or solar still.

One item you should be sure gets into the life raft is your vessel's EPIRB.

Other items, which normally will not be part of your abandon-ship bag but which you should try to grab if you have time, include your hand-held VHF radio (preferably in a waterproof container), any special medications or eyeglasses you require, your passport, and a few dollars in American currency. It's a good idea, in fact, for all members of the crew to keep special medications, eyeglasses, their passports, and a few greenbacks close by their bunks in a waterproof container that they can grab quickly on their way out.

If you can do so quickly, also grab additional flares or other signaling devices, water, provisions, and clothing.

SUGGESTED CONTENTS FOR ABANDON-SHIP BAG

SIGNALING EQUIPMENT

1 Class B mini-EPIRB (if no Class S EPIRB packed in life-raft canister)

3 SOLAS-type red parachute flares

3 SOLAS-type white parachute flares

3 SOLAS-type red hand-held flares

3 SOLAS-type orange smoke canisters

12 cylume chemical light sticks

1 waterproof flashlight with spare batteries

1 waterproof compass

1 signaling mirror

MEDICAL SUPPLIES

1 vial of seasickness pills

2 tubes of sunburn cream

1 jar of petroleum jelly

1 tube of antiseptic ointment

1 vial of prescription-strength pain pills

PROVISIONS

1 hand-operated watermaker or solar still

1 one-gallon folding plastic jug

2 packages high-energy freeze-dried food per person

CLOTHING/PERSONAL

1 long-sleeved shirt per person

1 sun visor or billed cap per person

1 pair of sunglasses per person

1 thermal blanket per person

2 rolls of toilet paper in self-sealing plastic bag

FISHING SUPPLIES

1 fillet knife in scabbard

1 spool thirty-pound test fishing line

20 feet of wire leader

3 medium fishing spoons

1 sixteen-inch spear gun

1 wire saw

2 propane cigarette lighters

Figure 1.2

• **Make certain life raft is tethered to vessel and launch it. In heavy seas, launch to leeward amidships.**

Ideally, your life raft will already be tethered to your vessel in its canister. If it's not and you fail to tether it, there is a good chance that it will be swept away by the sea. Launching your raft to leeward has several advantages, particularly if you are in a heavy sea. The inflation lanyard on most CO_2-equipped life rafts is 25 to 40 feet long and must be pulled out entirely before the life raft will inflate. Launching the life raft to leeward will carry it away from your vessel and speed the inflation process. A life raft launched to windward is likely to be blown up onto the vessel, making it difficult to board. As the sea causes the stern of the vessel to rise, a life raft launched to windward might become trapped under it and punctured by the rudder or propeller, or a heavy sea could drive the vessel down on the life raft. To avoid that, do not pull the life raft's tether line up tightly to your vessel but leave two to three feet of slack in it.

In a heavy sea, launching the life raft amidships positions it opposite the most stable part of the vessel, which makes it easier to board and provides a bit of protection from the weather in the lee of the vessel's doghouse or superstructure.

Once you have launched the raft, one crew member should steady it while a second crew member boards. If you have time, the crew member in the life raft should release the heaving line attached to the side of the raft and throw it back to a crew member on deck. The tether line should then be slackened and the life raft lashed alongside the vessel by its tether and the heaving line, attached to your vessel at angles of approximately 45 degrees (fig. 1.3). This will make the life raft more stable and easier to board and load. Again, leave enough slack in the lines to allow the life raft to ride two to three feet to leeward of your vessel's hull.

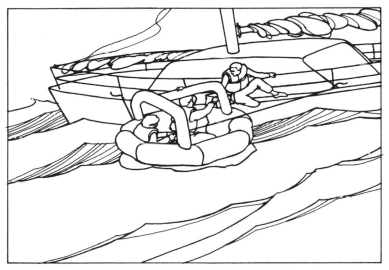

Figure 1.3 Launching a life raft to leeward positions it in the wind shadow of the main vessel. Launching the raft amidships positions it at the main vessel's most stable point.

- **Load crew and emergency supplies into life raft.**

Load the rest of your crew into the life raft and have them fend it off from your vessel while you load your emergency gear, to avoid snagging the life raft on anything that might puncture it. If at all possible, the crew should step or jump directly from your vessel into the life raft rather than jumping into the water and then trying to crawl up into it. If you can accomplish this maneuver, you lessen the danger of crew members being swept away from the raft. In cold waters, you also reduce the danger of their suffering the effects of hypothermia.

- **Activate EPIRB and fire one red meteor or parachute flare.**

A Class A EPIRB and a Type 406 Category 1 EPIRB are automatically activated by immersion in water. A Class S EPIRB packed inside a life raft is automatically activated when the life raft inflates. Class B, mini-B, and C EPIRBs and Type 406 Category 2 EPIRBs must be manually activated. Make certain your EPIRB is securely attached to your life raft and activate it as soon as you enter the raft.

Class C EPIRBs are intended only for inland or inshore use. They broadcast distress signals only on 156.75 MHz (VHF Channel 15) and 156.8 MHz (VHF Channel 16), which cannot be picked up by the COSPAS/SARSAT satellites or by overflying aircraft but only by VHF radios. Their maximum range is advertised as twenty miles, but with their antennae so close to the water, it is doubtful that their signals will reach that far under any but ideal conditions.

Class A, B, mini-B, and S EPIRBs broadcast distress signals on 121.5 MHz and 243.0 MHz. Their 121.5 MHz signals are monitored by over-flying commercial aircraft and may be received by the COSPAS/SARSAT satellites. Their 243.0 MHz signal can be received by only a few of the COSPAS/SARSAT satellites and certain military aircraft. There are several limitations on the operations of these EPIRBs of which you should be aware. Their 121.5 MHz signal, for example, is subject to interference; it may not be compatible with the COSPAS/SARSAT satellites; and sources other than EPIRBs transmit on that frequency, which can make identification of an actual distress signal difficult. In order for the COSPAS/SARSAT satellites to pick up a signal from one of these EPIRBs and relay it to a ground receiving station, the satellite must be in view of the EPIRB and the receiving station simultaneously. There are major areas of the world's oceans where this is not possible. Even if you must abandon ship in an area not covered by the satellites, however, the Coast Guard recommends that you activate your Class A, B, mini-B, or S EPIRB as soon as you leave your vessel in the hope that its signal may be picked up by over-flying commercial or military aircraft.

Both categories 1 and 2 of Type 406 EPIRBs broadcast distress signals on 406 MHz and 121.5 MHz. The 406 MHz component of signals broadcast by the Type 406 EPIRBs can be received and stored by the COSPAS/SARSAT satellites, then relayed when the satellite comes into view of a ground receiving station (fig. 1.4). Thus, the coverage of Type 406 EPIRBs is worldwide. The 121.5 MHz component of Type 406 EPIRB signals is also monitored by commercial aircraft and can be used by rescuers as a homing signal.

It makes sense to fire a red meteor or parachute flare as soon as you depart your vessel. In heavily traveled areas, there is a reasonable chance that it will be sighted by a nearby vessel. Even in remote areas, there is always the possibility that it will be spotted by a vessel out of your line-of-sight over the horizon or obscured by darkness or weather, and that the vessel will come into your vicinity to investigate its source. Do not fire any other flares until rescuers are within sight or hearing distance.

- **Keep life raft tethered to main vessel for as long as possible.**

If your vessel is afire or about to sink, you will have to cut the lines tethering the life raft to it. But if it is merely awash, keep the life raft tethered to it as long as possible. (In heavy seas, free the heaving line and pay out the full length of the life raft's tether to keep the raft away from your main vessel and avoid its being trapped beneath it or punctured.) You may be

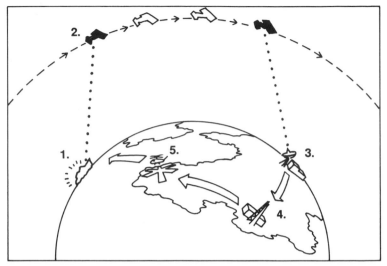

Figure 14 Distress signals from Type 406 Emergency Position Indication Radio Beacons can be stored aboard COSPAS/SARSAT satellites for relay to ground recieving stations, making the system's coverage worldwide.

able to go back aboard for other provisions you were unable to get into the life raft when you abandoned ship, and even an awash vessel is a larger target to spot than a lone life raft.

Tips on Life Raft Survival

If you should ever have the misfortune to find yourself adrift at sea in a life raft for an extended period of time, here are the tough realities of some of the problems you would face and several suggestions that might increase your chances of surviving the ordeal:

• No matter how tantalizingly close land may seem to be, NEVER leave the life raft and try to swim for shore.

Distances over water are deceptive and your goal almost inevitably will be much farther away than you think it is. You may well be in a severely weakened physical, and perhaps mental, state, and find that you are unable to swim even a short distance that you could handle easily under more normal circumstances. You may also expose yourself to the dangers of hypothermia and attack by sharks.

• Assume that rescue, if it comes at all, will come later rather than sooner.

Don't delude yourself into thinking that just because you activated a Class A, B, mini-B, or S EPIRB help is on the way. The 121.5 MHz of some EPIRBs are not compatible with the satellites; you may be out of the COSPAS/SARSAT coverage area; and over-flying aircraft may not be monitoring the frequencies on which your EPIRB is transmitting.

Even if your Class A, B, mini-B, or S EPIRB signal does reach the Coast Guard, there are several reasons they are not likely to launch a full air-sea rescue search for you immediately. First is that over 90 percent of the distress signals the Coast Guard receives from both marine EPIRBs and their close cousins, the Emergency Location Transmitters carried aboard aircraft, turn out to be false alarms due to the unit being activated accidentally. (Of the 7,700 alerts the Coast Guard receives over 121.5 MHz in a typical quarter, it ultimately determines the source of only about 220—less than 3 percent. Of those 220 cases where it is able to identify the source of the alert, only about fourteen turn out to be genuine distress situations.) A second reason is that the Coast Guard's expanded responsibilities for illegal drug interdiction have strained its resources, and it may not have crew or equipment available to deploy immediately. A third reason is that the Coast Guard is under tremendous pressure to hold down its expenses (it now costs some $7 thousand per hour to operate a C-130 air-sea rescue aircraft). For all these reasons, the Coast Guard has an extensive—and time-consuming—list of procedures it goes through to try to confirm that a signal from a Class A, B, mini-B or S EPIRB represents a genuine emergency. Even if the Coast Guard receives a 121.5 MHz distress alert that was relayed from a satellite, in the absence of other corroborating evidence of an actual distress, such as receipt of a distress call over VHF or SSB radio or receipt of the EPIRB signal by an over-flying aircraft, it normally will wait for verification by a second satellite pass before it launches a search, and that can take up to two hours. For these reasons, the average time between the receipt of a distress signal from one of these EPIRBs and the commencement of a full-scale air-sea rescue effort is twenty-six hours!

Once a full air-sea search is initiated, the rescuers still have to find you. If your Class A, B, mini-B, or S EPIRB signal is picked up by a satellite, it provides a fix which is accurate only within 10 to 20 nautical miles. If its signal is picked up by a lone aircraft flying overhead at 35,000 feet—a typical altitude for over-water flights—that single fix is accurate only to within 25 to 30 nautical miles, which still leaves rescuers a lot of ocean to cover.

You can improve your chances of rescue considerably by using one of the new Type 406 EPIRBs. The Coast Guard responds much more rapidly to distress alerts received from this type of EPIRB because the 406 MHz component of its signal transmits a 121-bit serial number that is distinctive to a particular unit. For Type 406 EPIRBs registered in the U.S.A., the Coast Guard can use that serial number to access a computer at Suitland, Maryland, operated by the National Oceanic and Atmospheric Administration (NOAA) that stores information about the vessel aboard which that EPIRB is carried. With that information, they can check with the vessel's owner or the owner's representative to confirm that the vessel is in fact in the vicinity from which the signal was received.

A Type 406 signal received by a COSPAS/SARSAT satellite significantly narrows the search area, as it provides a fix accurate to within 1.5 to 3 nautical miles.

- Ration your water and provisions on the assumption of an extended stay at sea.

Those who have spent long periods adrift at sea on a life raft say that for the first few days it is fairly easy to ration food and water. After about a week, however, it is too easy to convince yourself that you might as well go ahead and eat and drink everything you have on board because if you save it, you won't live long enough to benefit from it.

As we said above, fresh water will be your most precious commodity. Half a cup of fresh water or other liquid per person every twenty-four hours is about the minimum required to sustain life over an extended period. On that basis, a half-gallon of water per person lasts for only a little over two weeks, after which a hand-held reverse-osmosis watermaker or a solar still becomes indispensable.

Never drink unpurified seawater. The salt it contains leads only to faster dehydration and eventual death.

- Depression will be your most deadly enemy.

No matter how long your ordeal lasts, you must keep up your spirits at all cost. Think of home, family, and friends. If you are religious, think of your God. When hopelessness starts to close in, exert all your strength to shove it out of your mind.

One of the earliest signs of depression is disinterest in food. If you encounter that in any of your crew, you must force him or her to eat. Failure to do so will only hasten death.

- In cold water, hypothermia will be your second most dangerous enemy.

In a survival situation in cold waters, do everything you can to conserve body heat. Remain as much as possible in a fetal position and use the available clothing to cover your head and crotch, the two areas most susceptible to the loss of body heat.

- In tropical waters, sharks will be your third worst enemy.

Bill and Simone Butler survived for sixty-six days in a life raft after their sailboat was rammed by whales and sank 1,200 miles off the coast of Central America. "We were attacked by thirty to forty sharks a day," Bill told me after they were rescued. "They didn't attack the raft with their teeth but butted it with their heads. They would slam into us at bullet-speed, then flip over on their backs and spray the raft with urine. They could spray urine eight, ten, fifteen feet into the air. To finish off the attack, they'd give the raft a great slap with their tails."

- Fish and turtles are your most likely source of life-sustaining protein.

In the open ocean, sea creatures tend to congregate in the shadow of any bit of flotsam they come across—such as your life raft. Bill and Simone Butler survived their ordeal largely because of the four to five hundred pounds of fish, mostly trigger fish, that Bill was able to catch. In one instance, Bill was able to catch a small turtle and wrestle it into the raft. In another, a marauding undersea predator drove a school of flying fish to the surface near the raft, and Bill was able to catch four of them by hand.

The fishing supplies you include in your abandon-ship bag, including artificial and preserved baits, can well provide the critical margin between life and death.

- Sea birds can be your second most valuable food resource.

Sea birds frequently alight on life rafts and can be caught if you move quickly. Their flesh provides both edible protein and a valuable source of bait to catch other sea creatures

Tips on Air-Sea Rescue

Rescue by Commercial Vessels and Aircraft

Within twelve hours after Bill and Simone Butler's boat sank out from under them, a commercial vessel came within a quarter of a mile of their life raft but never spotted them. Commercial vessels are required to keep a lookout posted at all times but are notorious for failing to do so.

If you are adrift in a raft and spot a vessel or low-flying aircraft in your vicinity during the day or hear its engines at night, fire off a red meteor or parachute flare. If it's daytime, wave your arms at your sides, preferably holding some bright article of clothing in each hand. If the sun is shining, use a signal mirror. In the case of an aircraft that's not actually searching for you, you'll probably get only one brief chance to attract the attention of its crew. In the case of a vessel, if you managed to get your VHF radio aboard the raft, transmit a Mayday call over Channel 16. (Do not point the radio's antenna at the ship but hold it straight up; radio waves radiate from an antenna in concentric circles.) If you spot a ship and signal to it but after about fifteen minutes it does not alter course in your direction, fire one more flare, transmit one more Mayday if possible, and continue to wave or flash your signal mirror. If you get no response after that, it's likely they have no lookout or radio watch posted and further efforts on your part are probably useless. In any case, don't make the mistake of draining your hand-held VHF radio's battery or firing all your flares in a single encounter. You may need both desperately if you come within range of another low-flying aircraft or a commercial vessel that is maintaining a lookout.

Rescue by U.S. Coast Guard Ships and Aircraft

The Coast Guard conducts air-sea search and rescue efforts with cutters or smaller vessels, fixed-wing aircraft such as the C-130, and helicopters. Its H-3 helicopters are designed to fly a maximum of 300 miles from shore, loiter for a maximum of twenty minutes to effect a pickup, then return to shore.

As soon as you see or hear the engines of a Coast Guard vessel, fixed-wing aircraft, or helicopter, fire off a red or white meteor or parachute flare if you have one. In the case of an aircraft, aim the meteor in front of it; they are virtually blind to the rear. As a second choice, in daylight fire a hand-held red flare or orange smoke canister, use a signal mirror if the sun is shining, and wave your arms at your sides; at night, fire a hand-held flare or activate your personal rescue or man overboard light. If you managed to get a hand-held VHF radio aboard your raft, turn it on and broadcast a Mayday distress message on Channel 16, remembering to hold the radio straight up.

If the Coast Guard spots you, what happens from that point on will depend primarily on the type of search-and-rescue craft that has located you and the state of the weather at the time.

If you are located by a Coast Guard ship and the sea is calm, it will probably just come alongside your life raft and take you aboard. If a heavy sea is running, the cutter is more likely to launch a rescue team in one of its small boats (probably a rigid-bottom inflatable) to come and get you.

If you are located by a helicopter and it approaches you, stay as near as possible to the center of your life raft and hang on to it tightly, as the helicopter rotors' strong down-draft can flip it over. If the weather conditions are at all manageable, the helicopter's crew probably will lower a rescue sling, basket, net, or seat. If you are not able to communicate with them via a hand-held VHF radio, use hand signals: arms horizontal and thumbs down to tell them to lower the conveyance; arms raised vertically and thumbs pointed up to tell them to hoist it. If those aboard the life raft are able to get into or onto whichever conveyance that is offered, see that they do so one at a time. If anyone on board the raft is not physically able to manage the transfer, one of the helicopter crew will probably enter the water to assist you. If anyone on the raft is seriously injured, the crew will probably lower a rescue litter to hoist the victim aboard.

If you are located by a C-130, it will circle around you and wiggle its wings to let you know that you have been spotted. If you do not have an operable hand-held VHF radio aboard, it will probably drop you a package containing one, along with other survival supplies. If that is necessary, the aircraft normally will approach your raft from downwind at an altitude of about 300 feet, drop the package about 100 feet from you, then continue to pay out a 200 to 300-foot lanyard attached to the package, which they will try to drop right on top of, or to windward of, you so that it will drift down across your raft. A C-130 cannot effect a pickup at sea but will radio your position to the nearest Coast Guard ship or helicopter in your vicinity. It can stay aloft for up to 14 hours and normally will circle your position as long as its fuel supply allows. As its fuel begins to run low, it may be replaced on station by a second aircraft. If it must leave you, don't panic. It has relayed your position to a helicopter or ship that can pick you up. Help is definitely on the way, but it may take it a while to arrive. If you are out of range of a helicopter and have to wait for a ship to pick you up, it will be steaming toward you at only about ten knots, so be patient and hang on.

CHAPTER TWO

FIRE

ENGINE-ROOM FIRE

- Shut off all engines, generators, and fans sharing the engine space involved with the fire.

- Close any open engine-room doors or hatches.

- If engine-room fire extinguisher system has not discharged automatically, activate it manually.

- Order trained crew member to stand by life raft and prepare to launch it. Order crew into life jackets.

- Transmit Mayday distress call and message or Pan-Pan urgency call and message.

- If engine-room fire extinguisher has discharged, keep all engine-room doors and hatches closed for 15 minutes before opening.

- Use portable fire extinguisher appropriate to type of material that is burning.

- If you must open a door or hatch behind which fire may be burning, have appropriate-type portable fire

CONTINUED

extinguisher ready, open door slowly, stay as low as possible, and keep door or hatch between yourself and the possible fire.

• Aim stream of portable fire extinguisher at base of flames, not flames themselves.

• Allow engine-room where CO_2 fire-extinguishing system has discharged to ventilate for 15 minutes before entering.

GALLEY FIRE

• Extinguish with type A/B extinguisher. Aim stream at base of flames, not flames themselves.

• If no extinguisher is available, use materials at hand, such as baking soda or a water-soaked towel. Water will put out alcohol fire but may spread flames of a very large fire to other combustible materials.

• Make sure propane supply is turned off at source.

ELECTRICAL FIRE

• Extinguish with type C extinguisher.

• If possible, restrict fire's access to oxygen.

• Never use water.

CONTINUED

FIRE IN ACCOMMODATIONS

- Extinguish with type A extinguisher.

- Flood base of fire with water.

- If possible, restrict fire's access to oxygen.

- If you must open a door or hatch behind which fire may be burning, have type A portable fire extinguisher ready, open door slowly, stay as low as possible, and keep door or hatch between yourself and possible fire.

FIRE ON DECK

- If fueled by a petroleum product, extinguish with type B extinguisher.

- If fueled by such combustible materials as wood, paper, or fabric, extinguish with type A extinguisher or water.

- If possible, jettison burning material overboard.

ENGINE-ROOM FIRE

- **Shut off all engines, generators, and fans sharing the engine space involved with the fire.**

When a turbo-charger fire erupted in the starboard engine of my friend Sumner Pingree's 53-foot sportfisherman, *Roulette*, off the coast of Puerto Rico, he did what most of us would have done. "I pulled the port engine back to idle while I went below to assess the damage," he told me later. "I didn't turn it off because I was afraid I might need it to get back to shore on. The Halon™ system had discharged and put the flames out. But when we opened the engine-room door, the fire reignited with a whoosh."

What Sumner didn't realize was that the idling port engine was sucking the fire suppressant chemical out of the engine-room, and at the same time sucking fresh oxygen into the engine-room to refuel the fire. This created the perfect conditions for the fire to reignite.

Shutting off all engines and generators that share the engine space involved with the fire also helps to close off any supplies of fuel or lubricating oils that might be fueling the flames. Shutting off any fans that share engine space involved with the fire prevents them from sucking in outside air to dilute the fire suppressant.

- **Close any open engine-room doors or hatches.**

A fire cannot continue to burn without oxygen. Shutting any open engine-room doors or hatches will help starve the fire of oxygen and snuff it out.

- **If engine-room fire extinguisher system has not discharged automatically, activate it manually.**

Automatic engine-room fire extinguishers normally are quite dependable and discharge as soon as a fire raises the temperature in the engine-room to their activation point. But like anything else mechanical, particularly in the corrosive marine environment, they can malfunction. If you see or smell smoke in the vicinity of your engine-room and your fire extinguisher system has not discharged automatically, activate it manually. Your vessel should have manual activation levers in the salon, at the flying bridge, wheelhouse and/or cockpit steering station, and in its below-decks accommodations.

- **Order trained crew member to stand by life raft and prepare to launch it. Order crew into life jackets.**

"Ten minutes after we realized we had a fire on board, we were swimming," Sumner Pingree told me after his harrowing experience aboard *Roulette*. "I was amazed at how quickly she burned."

Because of the presence of highly flammable liquids such as diesel fuel or gasoline and lubricating oils, any engine-room fire has the potential to destroy a vessel in minutes. The resins used in most modern fiberglass yachts are themselves highly flammable and can quickly turn into a raging inferno.

The moment you realize that you have an engine-room fire aboard your vessel, take the precautions of ordering a crew member to stand by the life raft and prepare to launch it and order your crew into their life jackets. If you are able to bring the fire under control quickly, you can order a standdown and will have lost nothing. If the fire gets out of hand and you must abandon ship, you will at least be that much further along in your preparations.

- **Transmit Mayday distress call and message or Pan-Pan urgency call and message.**

The instant Sumner Pingree realized that *Roulette's* engine-room was afire, he transmitted a Mayday. "After the fire reignited," he says, "I raced back up to the flying bridge to get off another call to the Coast Guard. In just those few minutes, the fire had burned through the battery cables, and the radio was dead."

Anytime you have fire break out in the engine-room, go ahead and transmit at least a Pan-Pan urgency call and message to alert potential rescuers that you may need their help. If the situation seems serious, you are fully justified in transmitting the Mayday distress call and message. Use the format detailed on page 178 and do not omit any items. If, by the time you get in contact with someone, you are not sure whether or not you will require assistance, have the person stand by while you assess the situation. If, while you are doing that, your radio is disabled, at least someone will be alerted to your problem and to your position.

- **If engine-room fire extinguisher has discharged, keep all engine-room doors and hatches closed for 15 minutes before opening.**

When Sumner Pingree opened the engine-room door to assess the damage caused by the fire aboard *Roulette*, he experienced what fire-fighting experts call a "reflash." The vessel's Halon system had extinguished the flames, but the metal parts of the engine had not cooled below the flash point of the turbo-charger lubricating oil that was fueling the fire. Opening the engine-room door admitted a fresh supply of oxygen and allowed the fire to reignite.

When you've got smoke billowing out of your engine-room and your automatic fire-extinguishing system has discharged, there is naturally a great temptation to yank open the engine-room door or hatch immediately to see what's going on. But don't do it! Wait at least 15 minutes to be sure the engine and any flammable material in the engine-room have cooled down to below the reflash point.

- **Use portable fire extinguisher appropriate to type of material that is burning.**

Type A portable extinguishers are intended primarily for use on fires fueled by such combustible materials as wood, paper, and textiles.

Type B portable extinguishers are intended primarily for use on fires fueled by petroleum products such as gasoline, diesel fuel, lubricating oil, and hydraulic fluid.

Type C portable extinguishers are intended primarily for use on electrical fires.

Some portable extinguishers carry dual ratings:

Type A/B portable extinguishers are effective against fires fueled by wood, paper, or textiles, and against fires fueled by petroleum products.

Type B/C portable extinguishers are effective against fires fueled by petroleum products and against electrical fires. These extinguishers are the type most often found on boats, because petroleum-based and electrical fires are the most common kinds of fires encountered afloat.

- **If you must open a door or hatch behind which fire may be burning, have appropriate-type portable fire extinguisher ready, open door slowly, stay as low as possible, and keep door or hatch between yourself and possible fire.**

Before opening any door or hatch that may have fire behind it, feel its exterior first. If it is too hot for you to hold your hand against, the fire probably is still burning. If your automatic fire-extinguishing system has discharged, wait for the engine-room to cool down. Even if the door or hatch is cool enough for you to hold your hand against it, have a portable fire-extinguisher ready for action and open the door cautiously. The door or hatch may be heavily insulated. Even if it is relatively cool, fire could be raging on the other side of it, or you could experience a reflash.

If your vessel is not equipped with an automatic fire-extinguishing system and you plan to try to put an engine-room fire out with a portable extinguisher, open the door cautiously, stay as low as possible since heat and flames tend to rise, and keep the door between yourself and the fire.

- **Aim the stream of portable fire-extinguisher at base of flames, not flames themselves.**

A fire extinguisher stream directed at the flames themselves does little good. You must aim the stream at the base of the fire to rob it of heat and oxygen at its source (fig. 2.1). Sweep the stream back and forth across the base of the fire until all flames are extinguished. Do not use short bursts of fire suppressant, as that gives the fire time to reignite between bursts. Once all flames are extinguished, stop discharging the extinguisher, but watch the area carefully for several moments in case the fire reignites.

- **Allow engine-room where CO_2 fire-extinguishing system has discharged to ventilate for 15 minutes before entering.**

In concentrations sufficient to choke off a fire, CO_2 is deadly. Once a CO_2 system has been discharged and you are sure the fire is out and the engine and any flammable liquids in it have cooled below the reflash point, open up the engine

Figure 2.1 *In fighting an engine-room fire, keep a hatch between yourself and the fire and aim the fire extinguisher's stream at the base of the fire rather than at the flames.*

space and allow it to ventilate for at least 15 minutes before you enter.

If you must enter an engine space where a CO_2 system has discharged before it has had time to ventilate (to rescue a person who was trapped in the space when the system discharged, for example), cover your mouth with a piece of fabric as a filter, hold your breath, and do not crouch down low any more than is absolutely necessary: CO_2 is heavier than air and will tend to sink towards the vessel's bilges.

Halon is also heavier than air and will sink into the vessel's bilges, but it is safe to breathe in the 5 to 7 percent concentrations normally used in automatic engine-room fire-extinguishing systems.

GALLEY FIRE

- **Extinguish with type A/B extinguisher. Aim stream at base of flames, not flames themselves.**

Galley fires are most likely to be fueled by flammable liquids such as grease, propane, or alcohol, or by combustible solid materials such as paper, wood, or fabric. A good type A/B extinguisher will be effective against both kinds of fires. Direct the extinguisher's stream at the base of the fire rather than at the flames themselves to rob the fire of heat and oxygen. Hold the stream steadily on the base of the flames until you are certain that the fire is out.

- **If no extinguisher is available, use materials at hand such as baking soda or a water-soaked towel. Water will put out alcohol fire but may spread flames of a very large fire to other combustible materials.**

Baking soda is a good dry chemical suppressant, as it robs the fire of oxygen. Rather than just dumping baking soda right out of the box, pour some in your hand, then broadcast it at the base of the flames. Be cautious about using water on alcohol fires. Water will extinguish a small alcohol fire but may spread the flames of a larger fire to other combustible materials.

Do not use water on grease fires. The grease will float on top of the water and can carry flames to other parts of the vessel, such as wood cabinetry and drapes.

- **Make sure propane supply is turned off at source.**

Most galleys that use propane for cooking are equipped with an electronic control that allows you to turn off the propane at the tank. (The propane tank itself should be housed in its own, well-ventilated compartment on the vessel's exterior.) Unburned propane is heavier than air and will sink to the vessel's lowest point, where it could explode. If you extinguish a propane fire, be certain the propane is turned off at the tank so that unburned propane does not build up.

ELECTRICAL FIRE

• **Extinguish with approved type C extinguisher.**
A primary concern in fighting an electrical fire is that the suppressant itself not be a conductor of electricity. Type C fire extinguishers use chemicals that are not electrical conductors.

The suppressant used in foam-type extinguishers will corrode electronics; the suppressant used in CO_2 and Halon extinguishers will not.

• **If possible, restrict fire's access to oxygen.**
In most electrical fires, the initial combustible material is the insulation around the wiring itself. Fires in electrical-wiring insulation cannot sustain themselves without a great deal of oxygen. If your circuit panels are encased in a heavy metal box, in many cases closing the box will be sufficient to extinguish a fire.

• **Never use water.**
Water is a conductor of electricity. If you throw water on an electrical fire and are standing in water yourself, the electric power could be conducted through the water and it may electrocute you.

FIRE IN ACCOMMODATIONS

- **Extinguish with type A extinguisher.**

Fires in a vessel's accommodations will most often be type A
(that is, fueled by such combustible material as wood, paper,
or fabric). You should have a type A extinguisher mounted in
your accommodations where you and your crew can get to it
easily, even in the dark. Aim the extinguisher's stream at the
base of the fire rather than at the flames themselves, and hold
it there steadily until you are certain the fire is out. Fighting a
fire with bursts of suppressant allows the fire to reignite
between bursts.

- **Flood base of fire with water.**

If no type A fire extinguisher is available, use water, which is
an effective suppressant for type A fires.

- **If possible, restrict fire's access to oxygen.**

Type A fires cannot continue to burn without a generous
supply of oxygen. Robbing a fire of oxygen simply by closing
a door or hatch can often help snuff it out.

- **If you must open a door or hatch behind which fire may
  be burning, have portable type A fire-extinguisher
  ready, open door slowly, stay as low as possible, and
  keep door or hatch between yourself and possible fire.**

Before opening any door or hatch that may have fire behind
it, feel its exterior first. If it is too hot for you to hold your
hand against, the fire is probably still burning. If you plan to
try to put the fire out with a portable extinguisher, open the
door cautiously, stay as low as possible since heat and flames
tend to rise, and keep the door between yourself and the

possible fire. Aim the extinguisher's stream at the base of the fire, not at the flames themselves, and hold it steady until you are certain the fire is out.

FIRE ON DECK

- **If fueled by a petroleum product, extinguish with type B extinguisher.**

A common source of deck fires aboard yachts is the gasoline used to fuel the dinghy's outboard motor. Although Coast Guard regulations do not require that a fire extinguisher be carried in most dinghies, you should keep a type B extinguisher aboard and make certain it is nearby whenever you are handling gasoline.

- **If fueled by such combustible materials as wood, paper, or fabric, extinguish with type A extinguisher or water.**

Water is an excellent suppressant for extinguishing type A fires. You should always keep handy on deck a stout bucket with a rope tied to its handle that is long enough to allow you to scoop up water from over your vessel's side rails.

- **If possible, jettison burning material overboard.**

The closest water to extinguish a deck fire is normally the water on which your vessel is floating. If possible, use a dinghy oar, whisker pole, or other long object to push the burning material over the side.

Tips on Fire Prevention

• Frequently inspect fuel and lubricating-oil lines (including your vessel's fuel-fill lines) for signs of wear or chafe, and keep their fittings tight.

• Clean up all petroleum spills promptly and properly dispose of the petroleum product and the material with which you cleaned up the spill. Never allow oily rags or waste to accumulate in your engine space.

• Frequently inspect your vessel's electrical wiring for signs of wear or chafe, especially in areas where wiring passes through a bulkhead and below galley counters, where wiring can be chafed by shifting pots and pans.

• Make certain all electrical circuits are protected by fuses or circuit breakers, and never install on one circuit more equipment than the circuit's wire size can safely handle.

• Exercise special caution when fueling your vessel or its dinghy's outboard. Before pumping fuel, activate your engine-room blowers to ventilate engine space and ground the nozzle of the filling hose to your deck fitting to discharge static electricity.

• Make certain your vessel is equipped with the proper number and type of fire extinguishers and that they are appropriately located. In addition to a fixed automatic fire-extinguishing system in the engine-room, you should at a minimum have portable fire extinguishers of the proper type mounted outside the engine-room door or hatch, in the galley, in the wheelhouse and/or flying bridge, and in the below-decks accommodations.

CHAPTER THREE

GROUNDING

- Keep calm.

- Check for crew injuries.

- Check for damage to vessel's hull, steering, and propulsion system.

- If assistance is required, transmit Pan-Pan urgency signal.

- Determine which way deep water lies.

- Determine if tide is rising or falling.

- Determine if wind and current are carrying the vessel harder aground.

- Lessen draft.

- Try backing with sails and/or engine.

- Set kedge anchor towards deep water and keep rode taut.

- Attempt to kedge off.

- Attempt to pivot bow towards deep water.

- If extrication is impossible until tide change, protect hull with materials at hand.

- **Keep calm.**

Running aground can be a traumatic experience, particularly if the grounding is unexpected and your vessel has significant way on when it strikes the bottom. Regardless of the drama of the situation, you need to keep your wits about you. In some cases, doing the right thing quickly can free your vessel in moments; doing the wrong thing—or waiting too long to do the right thing—can expose your vessel to serious damage and your crew to possible injury. Panic reactions are only likely to get you in a worse predicament.

- **Check for crew injuries.**

When a sizable vessel strikes the bottom at even three or four knots, your crew can suffer bodily injuries as inertia slams them into bulkheads or tosses them from their bunks. Quickly assess any injuries to your crew to determine if any are serious enough to require an immediate call for assistance.

- **Check for damage to vessel's hull, steering, and propulsion system.**

In a hard grounding, keels, rudders, struts, and drive shafts can be torn away, leaving gaping holes in your vessel's hull. Quickly determine whether your vessel has suffered any severe threat to the integrity of its hull and if you therefore require immediate assistance. If your hull's integrity has been breached in the grounding, you may be better off allowing your vessel to remain grounded until you can make temporary repairs.

- **If assistance is required, transmit Pan-Pan urgency signal.**

If the tide is falling, if your vessel is banging on the rocks and is in danger of being holed, or if any of your crew were injured in the grounding, you're going to have to call for assistance. The correct procedure for doing that is to broadcast the Pan-Pan signal (see page 189).

- **Determine which way deep water lies.**

In warm tropical waters, go over the side to assess the situation at first hand. In cold or murky waters, take soundings around your vessel with a boat hook or whisker pole to figure out which way you need to move your vessel in order to get back to water she can float in.

- **Determine if tide is rising or falling.**

In tidal areas, the state of the tide at the time of a grounding is critical. If the tide is rising and your vessel is not actually banging on the bottom, you can afford to relax and let the tide come in and lift her free, unless the wind and current are in the direction of the obstruction (see next instruction). If the tide is falling, you must work quickly and purposefully if you are to free your vessel as the tide ebbs.

- **Determine if wind and current are carrying the vessel harder aground.**

After the state of the tide, wind and current will usually be the two most crucial elements in deciding whether you can free your vessel quickly or whether you will be left high and dry for hours. In either case, try to make the situation work for rather than against you. On a rising tide, if wind or current is in the direction of the obstruction, you should immediately set an anchor towards deep water to keep your vessel from going harder aground (Fig. 3.1). If wind or current is pushing your vessel towards deeper water, quickly back your sails or attempt to turn your powerboat's broad stern towards the wind or current to give it additional area to work against.

- **Lessen draft.**

If you're going to try to refloat the vessel yourself, lessen its draft any way you can. On a retractable keel sailboat, raise the keel and kick-up rudder. On smaller vessels, move weight and crew to the bow, which may create enough leverage to break the bottom suction. Rapidly shifting crew weight from side to side can often achieve the same result. On an out-drive or outboard-powered boat, raise the shafts. On a keel-type sailboat, set a kedge anchor off the deep-water beam, attach the main halyard to its rode, and use the main halyard winch to try to heel the boat over as much as possible.

- **Try backing with sails and/or engine.**

If your vessel doesn't seem to be hard aground and you are certain deeper water lies astern, try backing down with your engine. Before the attempt, check your engine's raw water strainers to make sure they were not clogged with sand or gravel when you went agroud. If they are obstructed, clean them out before starting the engine. Don't try that maneuver more than a couple of times, and then only for about a minute each time. You could easily suck sand or mud into the engine's raw water intake and cause the engine to overheat, which is only going to compound your woes. If you're on a sailboat and the wind is from forward of your beam, back your sails before you try to ease off with your engine.

One useful trick is to hail a passing powerboat and ask its skipper to intentionally rack your vessel's wake. The motion may break your vessel clear from the bottom and allow you to use your engine to back off.

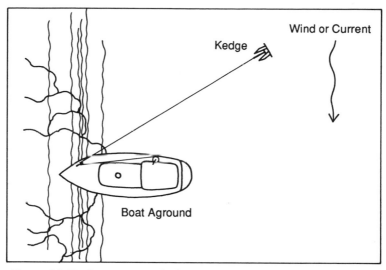

Figure 3.1 To pivot your vessel's bow in a grounding situation, set a kedge at 45 degrees to wind or current and lead its rode through a bow fairlead, then back to a cockpit winch.

Unless you're certain deep water lies ahead, it's not a good idea to try to go forward, since that's probably what got you into trouble in the first place.

• **Set kedge anchor towards deep water and keep rode taut.**

This will keep you from drifting up farther on whatever your vessel's keel is resting against.

• **Attempt to kedge off.**

With a sailboat, set a kedge anchor astern, rig a bridle to connect its rode to both sheet winches, and try to crank your way off.

- **Attempt to pivot bow towards deep water.**

If going astern doesn't work, the next step is to try to pivot your vessel to get her bow pointed back towards deep water. If you have a dinghy with a sizable engine, use it to try to pull her bow around. If not, set a kedge at 45 degrees to deep water and try to crank the bow around. Most electric anchor winches won't stand up to the strain this kind of maneuver puts on them. It's better to lead the kedge rode back to your main halyard or cockpit winches and use one of them.

- **If extrication is impossible until tide change, protect hull with materials at hand.**

If it becomes obvious that you're not going to get your vessel off the bottom until the tide floods, about all you can do is protect her hull as best you can until the rising tide refloats her. On a sailboat, keep tension on the rode of the kedge anchor you set out abeam and attached to your main halyard. On a sail- or powerboat, set boat hooks, whisker poles, or anything else you can lay your hands on against the sheer as braces (but pad them well). If she's about to lay on her chine or the turn of her bilge, pad it with any type of cushioning material you have on board.

Freeing with an Assisting Vessel

Here are some helpful tips for situations in which a second vessel is involved in trying to free a grounded vessel:

- Before approaching a grounded vessel, the captain of the assisting vessel must make certain that it is possible to assist without allowing his or her own vessel to become grounded.

- If yours is the vessel aground, to help avoid potential disputes over salvage rights it's best to pass your tow line to the assisting vessel rather than accepting a line from the vessel offering assistance (see "Legal Aspects of Providing and Accepting Assistance" below). To avoid the possibility of the tow line fouling the prop of the assisting vessel, bend a floating messenger line such as polypropylene ski rope onto your tow line, weight its bitter end, and heave it rather than the tow line. If the distance between your grounded vessel and the assisting vessel is too great to heave a messenger line, attach the tow line to your own vessel and ferry it over to the assisting vessel in your dinghy, allowing it to pay out as you go. If you have no dinghy, in warm waters you can swim the line over. Wear a life jacket, attach the tow line to your own vessel first and support it on a float, allowing it to pay out as you go. If the assisting vessel lies downwind and down current from you, attach a float to the tow line or a messenger line and allow it to float down to the other vessel.

- If yours is the assisting vessel and you must pass your tow line to the grounded vessel, make certain you can approach the grounded vessel close enough to heave the tow line or a messenger line without endangering your own vessel. If yours is a single-screw powerboat or a sailboat, it will be more maneuverable and its prop exposed to less danger if you approach the grounded vessel bow-on. If yours is a twin-screw powerboat that you are adept at handling in reverse, and the bottom poses no threat to your props, backing down on the grounded vessel will leave your bow pointed towards open water and put you in the proper position for making the tow.

If you cannot approach the grounded vessel close enough to heave a tow line or messenger line, row or swim the line over as above or attach a float to its bitter end, launch it up wind and up current of the grounded vessel, and allow it to float down to the vessel in distress.

• Once a tow line has been passed, the captains of both the grounded vessel and the assisting vessel should see that it is attached to the strongest point of their respective vessels. On many modern boats that point of attachment should not be a deck cleat, because they often are not strong enough to withstand the severe stresses involved in freeing a vessel that is hard aground. The same is often true of a sailboat's sheet winches. On a modern sailboat with a keel-stepped mast, the base of the mast normally will be the strongest point of attachment. On sailboats whose masts are not stepped to the keel, and on most powerboats, it normally is best to pass a line entirely around the doghouse, padding it heavily at the points of greatest stress.

• The propellers of all boats produce far more power going ahead than they do in reverse; therefore the bow of the assisting vessel should be pointed towards open water. While the assisting vessel is attempting to pull the grounded vessel free, its maneuverability will be severely restricted and provision must be made to keep the assisting vessel itself from being swept aground. If wind and current are striking the assisting vessel from other than abeam, the tow line should be rigged to the assisting vessel's stern and the pull made in a straight line. If wind and current are striking the assisting vessel on its beam, the tow line should be attached just aft of abeam on the upwind or up-current side to allow its bow to be headed into—or at least quarter to—wind and current (fig. 3.2).

In conditions of strong beam wind or current, the captain of the assisting vessel may need to set his or her own kedge to windward and have a crew member maintain a strain on the anchor line to help keep the vessel's bow from falling off and possibly allowing the vessel to be swept aground. The anchor winch, however, should be used only to help keep the bow of the assisting vessel into or quarter to wind and current. It should not be used to help exert pulling force itself, as it normally will not be strong enough to stand the strain involved.

• Before the attempt to free the grounded vessel begins, the captains of both the grounded vessel and the assisting vessel should have a clear channel for communicating

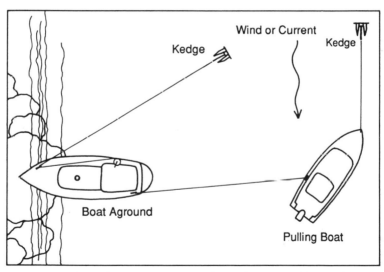

Figure 3.2 If vessel assisting in a grounding is being struck by wind or current abeam, it should set its own kedge directly toward the wind or current to keep its bow from falling off. Attaching the tow line to the assisting vessel just aft of abeam rather than at the stern will allow it more freedom to manuever.

with each other. Preferably it will be over a working VHF radio channel such as 6 or 68. If one or both vessels does not have a working VHF radio aboard, they should agree on a set of hand signals through which they can communicate.

- Before the towing operation commences, the crew of both vessels should stand well clear of the tow line. Under the pressure of towing, it can snap and lash back towards either vessel, causing severe injuries.

- Before the attempt to free the grounded vessel begins, its captain should make sure there is a kedge out and a crew member taking up slack in its line to keep the vessel from being swept back aground once it is freed. If the grounded vessel is without power, it's also a good idea to have a crew member ready to set a second anchor if necessary once the vessel is freed.

- During the towing maneuver itself, the captain of the assisting vessel should exert slow, steady pressure on the tow line, avoiding sudden accelerations, which can break the tow line or cause severe damage to one or both vessels.

Legal Aspects of Accepting and Providing Assistance

In most cases in which your vessel is aground, you can accept assistance from a fellow recreational boater without concern that he or she may lay claim to your vessel under maritime law pertaining to salvage rights. Maritime law on salvage rights is extremely ill-defined and by and large relates primarily to vessels that have been legally abandoned.

Usually, in order to claim salvage rights, the captain of a salvaging vessel must demonstrate that the vessel being claimed had been abandoned by its owner, who was making no attempt to salvage it. The fact that you are aboard the vessel and making an attempt to extricate it from danger is what lawyers call "proof on its face" that you had not abandoned it, and therefore the laws on rights of salvage do not apply.

In the absence of a contract, you also can accept assistance from a fellow recreational boater without undue concern that you will be charged an exorbitant fee for his or her services. Unless a price for services is stated before the attempt to free your vessel commences and you agree to pay the stated fee in front of witnesses, any subsequent attempts to charge you would fall under the "just and reasonable" concept. If the assisting boater were to take you to court, he or she might succeed in making you pay something, but any charges would have to be "just and reasonable" for the service performed. You could find that you are liable for any damages to the assisting vessel that resulted from the attempt to help you, but they would probably be covered by the liability clause of your boat-owner's insurance. Even if the assisting boater does state an unreasonable fee and you verbally agree to pay it in front of witnesses, most of the lawyers I've discussed the matter with say you could argue that the contact was made under duress, and a court would probably order you to pay only a fee which was "just and reasonable" for the service performed.

If you are dealing with a commercial towing service, however, the situation can be significantly different. Their representative, either the captain of the vessel they send to assist you or someone in their office you talk with over the radio, will clearly state a price and require that you agree to pay it before assistance commences. The prices some of these services charge are outrageous, but if you agree to their fee, you probably will have no choice but to pay it.

The hull insurance of a good yacht policy normally covers the cost of towing and assistance if it is required to keep the yacht from suffering further damage.

CHAPTER FOUR

HEAVY WEATHER

- At first signs of severe weather, dog all hatches, rig jack lines, order crew into life jackets, and break out safety harnesses.

- If you can reach safe harbor before storm's leading edge arrives and inlet can be run in adverse conditions, head inshore.

- If storm's leading edge is over inlet or inlet is dangerous in adverse weather, stay offshore until conditions moderate.

- In winds 30 to 40 knots and waves 15 to 18 feet, ride downwind, possibly streaming a warp, drogue, or storm anchor.

- In winds over 40 knots and waves over 18 feet, put your vessel's head to weather. Execute turn smartly and with extreme caution on back of seventh wave.

- In extreme weather, if piloting a sailboat, heave to or lie ahull, possibly streaming bow warp or anchor. If piloting a power vessel, maintain headway with wind 15 degrees off windward bow.

- At first signs of severe weather, dog all hatches, rig jack lines, order crew into life jackets, and break out safety harnesses.

Don't wait for conditions to get severe before you start taking the weather into account. For most of us, weather at sea becomes a concern when winds begin to build to around 30 knots and waves approach about 8 feet. If you find yourself in winds and waves approaching that magnitude, and weather reports indicate that conditions are likely to worsen, secure your vessel by closing and dogging all portholes and hatches, stowing or lashing down loose gear, and rigging jack lines, which will enable you and your crew to move fore and aft on deck safely using safety harnesses. Don your own life jacket and order your crew to do likewise. Also make sure your safety harnesses are accessible and do not allow any crew member to go forward on deck without wearing one and securing it to the jack lines.

- If you can reach safe harbor before storm's leading edge arrives and inlet can be run in adverse conditions, head inshore.

When bad weather hits, the first impulse of most of us is to head for shore. If you can reach safe harbor before conditions deteriorate further, and the inlet leading to safe harbor can be run in adverse conditions, heading in is normally the wisest choice.

- If storm's leading edge is over inlet or inlet is dangerous in adverse conditions, stay offshore until conditions moderate.

Bear in mind that a front's most violent weather is likely to be on its leading edge, that waters are rougher inshore than offshore because shallow water compacts and magnifies wave force, and that many inlets are extremely dangerous in adverse conditions, particularly at low tide. If you cannot reach the inlet leading to safe harbor before the storm's leading edge arrives, or if the inlet is dangerous to run in adverse weather, you generally will be better off remaining in deep water until conditions moderate. The wave action in deep water is likely to be less violent than closer inshore, and in deep water you are more likely to encounter the big rolling waves that stay together rather than more dangerous short, choppy waves with breaking tops. I was in the Abaco islands several years ago when a nor'easter created what the locals call a "rage," producing 20-foot waves across the bar of Whale Cay Passage. Despite radioed warnings from Bahamas Air-Sea Rescue not to attempt an entrance, the owners of a 52-foot sailboat tried to come in and their vessel was pitchpoled. The husband was killed and his wife seriously injured. Had they stayed in the relative safety of deep water until the rage died down, the man probably would have survived.

- **In winds 30 to 40 knots and waves 15 to 18 feet, ride downwind, possibly streaming a warp, drogue, or storm anchor.**

The most comfortable attitude in which to ride out winds of around 30 to 40 knots and waves of up to about 18 feet is running downwind. If you choose to bear off, make certain you keep your vessel running as straight as possible before wind and seas and be constantly alert to the possibility of a broach. Streaming a long, heavy warp, a drogue, or a storm anchor from the stern will help keep the stern into the wind and the bow pointed directly downwind to help you avoid a broach.

- **In winds over 40 knots and waves over 18 feet, put your vessel's head to weather. Execute turn smartly and with extreme caution on back of seventh wave.**

If winds continue to build to over about 40 knots and waves to over about 18 feet, the danger of a broach may make continuing downwind impossible. In that case, you are going to have to put your vessel's head to wind (Fig. 4.1). During the turn you must make to accomplish this, your boat's beam will be exposed to the storm's full fury and she will be at her most vulnerable. There are several specific techniques you can employ to make that turn as quickly and safely as possible.

First, the longer you wait to make the turn, the worse it will be. As soon as you experience significant difficulty in keeping your vessel's bow pointed dead downwind, go ahead and make plans to turn. Postponing the maneuver will only make it harder to accomplish.

Second, keep your cool. Scuba divers have a rule: plan your dive, and dive your plan. Mariners about to turn head-to-weather in storm conditions should have a similar rule: plan your turn, and turn your plan. Once you have your turn mapped out, follow your intentions through cleanly and smoothly. An instant's panic or hesitation could be disastrous.

Third, time your turn carefully. According to some oceanographers, waves tend to travel in series of seven, with every seventh wave tending to be smaller than the others, and the interval between it and the wave right behind it tending to be longer. That rule is not absolute, but in planning your turn observe the waves passing under your vessel and see if you can discern which in their series tends to be the smallest and has the longest period between it and the next wave. Plan to make your turn as soon as the crest of that smallest wave has passed under your vessel's keel.

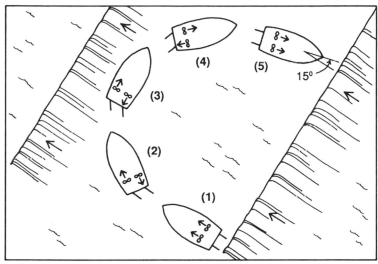

Figure 4.1 Turning a twin-engine displacement hull vessel head to wind in heavy seas should be executed by using its engines in addition to its steering. Once the decision to turn into the wind is made (1), turn both rudders in the direction of the wind and shift the windward engine into reverse (2). Maintain that condition (3, 4) until your bow is almost directly into the wind, then shift the windward engine back into forward gear (5). The vessel will ride most comfortably if it takes the wind about 15 degrees off its bow.

You want to make as much of your turn as possible on the back of that smallest wave, so that once you are into the trough behind it, your vessel is properly positioned to meet the next wave rushing towards you. Ideally, to reduce the likelihood of burying your bow into the base of that oncoming wave, it's best to meet it at an angle of about 15 degrees, with the wind remaining on the weather side of your bow. At this point, do not pass the bow through the wind.

If the period between waves is so short that you cannot possibly make the turn on the back of one wave, bear off about 20 degrees as you are lifted on the wave's face, then complete your turn once its crest has passed beneath you.

In a single-engine powerboat or a sailboat, about all you can do to get your vessel through the turn as quickly as possible is to put your wheel over hard to windward (or your sailboat's tiller hard alee) and increase engine rpm.

If you are in a twin-screw powerboat, you can use its engines to even greater advantage. In a planing hull motor yacht, you normally can accomplish the turn quickly by leaving both engines in forward gear, increasing their power slightly, and turning the wheel sharply to windward. With a displacement vessel, you may find it necessary to put the windward engine in reverse (while leaving the leeward engine in forward gear), then increase rpms on both engines to swing her bow around quickly.

Regardless of the type of vessel, just be sure you don't apply too much power. You could drive your vessel down the back of the wave so rapidly that you bury her bow in the base of the oncoming wave.

Once you are successful in getting your vessel's head to weather, she probably will ride most comfortably if you continue to take oncoming waves at about 15 degrees off the bow rather than from dead ahead. Just be alert to the danger that an especially large wave could knock her so far off her track that her beam is exposed to the storm's full fury.

- **In extreme weather, if piloting a sailboat, heave to or lie ahull, possibly streaming bow warp or anchor. If piloting a power vessel, maintain headway with wind 15 degrees off windward bow.**

Sailboats can often weather horrendous storms by simply heaving to or lying ahull. The specifics of heaving to vary greatly due to a sailboat's design and the strength of the wind. Some boats require a storm jib and/or storm trysail to

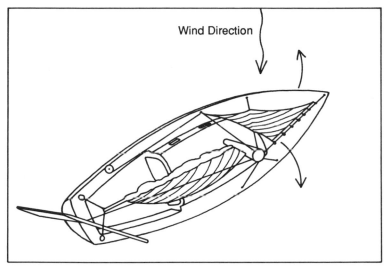

Wind Direction

Figure 4.2 The basic procedure for heaving to in a sailboat is accomplished by deeply reefing or furling the mainsail, sheeting the jib to weather and lashing the rudder to windward. The counter-balancing forces of the jib and the rudder should allow the vessel to ride with her bow about 45 degrees off the wind while making only gradual leeway.

execute the maneuver satisfactorily. To accomplish the basic procedure (Fig. 4.2), deeply reef or furl the mainsail, sheet the jib to weather, allow the bow to fall off, and lash the wheel to windward (or the tiller to the vessel's leeward side). The position of the jib will tend to keep the vessel's bow off the wind, while the position of the tiller will want to turn her bow into the wind. The resulting counterforces should balance the vessel in equilibrium and leave it riding with its bow about 45 degrees off the wind, making only gradual leeway. If a lee shore poses a potential danger, you can reduce leeway even more by streaming a long, heavy warp or a storm anchor from the bow. However, most bow cleats will not stand the strain of a warp or storm anchor. On a vessel with a mast stepped to its keel, secure the bitter end of the warp or the storm anchor's rode to the base of the mast, then lead it through a bow fairlead to keep it in position. If a sailboat's mast is stepped on the cabin top, pass the bitter end of the warp or the storm anchor's rode around the entire house and pad it carefully at the points of greatest stress.

To lie a-hull, remove all sails, lash the rudder to the windward, and allow the vessel to see to herself.

In extreme weather, a powerboat must maintain headway. If caught without headway, she will eventually lie with her beam to wind and waves. Powerboats lying in this position are extremely vulnerable to structural damage because most of them present a significant profile against which the wind can exert its capsizing force, most lack a significant keel or ballast to help keep them upright, and many have vast expanses of salon glass that can be caved in by the force of green water. A powerboat headed to weather will ride most comfortably with just enough speed on to maintain steerage and keep the wind about 15 degrees off the windward side of her bow.

CHAPTER FIVE

HELICOPTER EVACUATION

- Request helicopter evacuation only in cases of life threatening emergency.

- To request helicopter evacuation, contact U.S. Coast Guard on VHF Channel 16 or SSB frequency 2182 kHz, then shift to assigned working frequency. Monitor assigned frequency until evacuation is completed.

WHILE HELICOPTER IS EN ROUTE:

- Prepare victim for evacuation.

- Clear evacuation path.

- Clear hoist area. If nighttime, prepare to light up hoist area and any obstructions.

- Make sure locating devices such as flares, smoke bombs, or signal lights are immediately accessible and ready for operation.

- Order crew into life jackets, assign specific duties, and arrange hand signals for communication.

CONTINUED

AFTER HELICOPTER ARRIVES:

- Reduce vessel speed to minimum required to maintain steerage. If pickup to be made from vessel's stern, put wind 30 degrees on port bow; if from vessel's bow, put wind 30 degrees on starboard bow.

- Once preparations for receiving litter are complete, signal helicopter to lower it with "thumbs down". Trail line from helicopter can be handled safely; allow litter to touch deck and discharge static electricity before handling.

- Allow all lines from helicopter to run free; do not attach them to vessel in any manner and keep all crew clear. Do not move litter from hoist area without detaching it from hoist cable.

- Load patient in litter and strap in. If necessary, reattach litter to hoist cable.

- Signal helicopter to hoist litter with "thumbs up" signal.

- During hoisting, steady litter to keep it clear of obstructions. Use trail line to steady litter until it is clear of vessel.

- **Request helicopter evacuation only in cases of life-threatening emergency.**

Evacuation of an injured person from a vessel by helicopter can be dangerous for the victim, the vessel's crew, and the helicopter crew, and should be initiated only in cases of life-threatening injury.

The H-3 rescue helicopters used by the Coast Guard are designed to fly a maximum of 300 nautical miles seaward from the closest refueling point, loiter over a vessel for a maximum of 20 minutes, then return to land. Coast Guard rescue helicopters normally do not conduct rescue operations in conjunction with the U.S. Navy.

- **To request helicopter evacuation, contact U.S. Coast Guard on VHF Channel 16 or SSB frequency 2182 kHz, then shift to assigned working frequency. Monitor assigned frequency until evacuation is completed.**

Once you reach the Coast Guard on VHF 16 or SSB 2182 kHz, they usually will instruct you to shift to a working channel. In rescue situations, that channel will most often be VHF Channel 22A or SSB Channel 2670 kHz. Once helicopter evacuation is agreed upon, it's imperative that you, or a crew member you assign to the task, monitor the working frequency until the evacuation is complete.

While the helicopter is en route, the coast station or the helicopter pilot normally will request a description of your vessel, information regarding your vessel's position, particulars of the hoist area aboard, and the winds, weather, and state of the sea in your vicinity. He or she will also brief you on any locating signals that will be required and on the pickup procedure itself.

WHILE HELICOPTER IS EN ROUTE:

• **Prepare victim for evacuation.**

Tag the victim with a brief description of the injury sustained or the symptoms he or she has shown and list any medications you have administered or procedures you have performed. If the victim is unconscious, include his or her name, age, next of kin, where next of kin can be reached by telephone, and the victim's blood type, if known.

In cold weather, if injuries permit, the victim should be dressed warmly, but avoid loose-fitting clothing or headgear, as this could become entangled in the hoisting equipment. If injuries permit, the victim should also be fitted with a life jacket.

• **Clear evacuation path.**

To avoid exposure to the weather, it's best if you can keep the victim inside the vessel until the helicopter arrives, but clear a wide, unobstructed path between the holding area inside and the hoist area on deck. If possible, it's also best to load the victim into the litter at the hoist area on your vessel. If the nature of the injuries requires you to bring the litter inside the vessel to load the victim, you need to clear an unobstructed path that will admit a rigid litter approximately 7 feet long by 2 1/2 feet wide.

• **Clear hoist area. If nighttime, prepare to light up hoist area and any obstructions.**

On a sailboat, the preferred hoist area will be the cockpit. If possible, remove the boom and mainsail and stow them forward. If the boom cannot be removed, furl the mainsail, swing the boom as far as possible to one side, and lash it securely to an aft lower shroud. If possible, detach the backstay and temporarily reattach it as far forward as possible. Remove or lower and secure any bimini tops or awnings that cover the cockpit. Also, stow any loose articles, which might be blown around by the wash from the helicopter's rotor.

On a large powerboat, the preferred hoist area is usually its highest and aft-most deck, which in most cases will be the cabin top. If the cabin top is normally used to stow the dinghy, launch the dinghy, if possible, and tow it astern on a long painter. Also lower and secure any bimini tops on the upper deck and any masts and/or antennae that will not be needed to communicate with the coast station or the helicopter.

If the evacuation must be conducted at night, arrange to light the hoist area and any obstructions with spreader lights and/or hand-held flashlights. Hand-held flashlights must, however, always be focused on the hoist area or any obstructions and not pointed towards the helicopter as they could temporarily blind the pilot.

- **Make sure locating devices such as flares, smoke bombs, or signal lights are immediately accessible and ready for operation.**

Once the helicopter reaches your vicinity, the pilot may request that you fire a flare or activate other locating devices to help pinpoint your position. Make certain your flare kit, spotlight, and any other signal devices you have on board are accessible and ready for service, but do not fire a flare unless requested to do so by the helicopter pilot or the coast station.

• **Order crew into life jackets, assign specific duties, and arrange hand signals for communication.**

You and all members of your crew should put on life jackets before the helicopter arrives. This includes crew members who are assigned to stay inside the vessel, as their presence might be needed on deck. Assign each member of the crew specific duties, such as taking over the helm and the radio, lighting the hoist area and any obstructions, receiving the litter on deck, getting the patient to the hoist area, and steadying the litter as it is hoisted into the helicopter.

Once the helicopter arrives overhead, the noise from its rotors will be deafening and normal spoken communication will be impossible. Agree on a simple set of hand signals for such commands as "Wait," "Go back," "Come on" and "OK." The accepted signal for the helicopter to lower the litter is to hold both arms out horizontally, with fists clenched and thumbs pointed downward (fig. 5.1). The accepted signal for the helicopter to hoist the litter is to hold both arms above the horizontal with fists clenched and thumbs pointed upward.

AFTER HELICOPTER ARRIVES:

• **Reduce vessel speed to minimum required to maintain steerage. If pickup is to be made from vessel's stern, put wind 30 degrees on port bow; if from vessel's bow, put wind 30 degrees on starboard bow.**

Due to the counterclockwise rotation of the helicopter's rotor, it is most maneuverable when the wind strikes it from ahead or on the starboard forward quarter. Helicopter pilots normally fly from the starboard seat and will want to put the starboard forward quarter of their craft towards your vessel for maximum visibility.

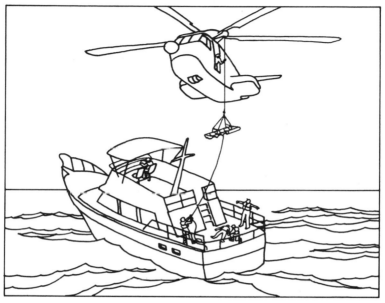

Figure 5.1 In executing an evacuation by helicopter, guide the litter to your vessel's deck using the trail line, but never attach the trail line to your vessel or allow it to become entangled with your vessel in any manner. Instruct the helicopter's hoist operator to lower the litter by fully extending your arms sideways and turning your thumbs downward.

- **Once preparations for receiving litter are complete, signal helicopter to lower it with "thumbs down". Trail line from helicopter ¸can be handled safely; allow litter to touch deck and discharge static electricity before handling.**

Often, the helicopter's hoist person will first lower a trail line, which will be attached to the bottom of the litter and will allow your crew to guide the litter to the hoist area. This line will be non-static and can be handled safely. But when the litter approaches your vessel, allow it to touch the deck and discharge any static electricity before handling it.

- **Allow all lines from helicopter to run free; do not attach them to vessel in any manner and keep all crew clear. Do not move litter from hoist area without detaching it from hoist cable.**

At no point in the evacuation should the helicopter be attached to your vessel by either the trail line or the hoist line. Make sure that neither becomes entangled with any part of your vessel and warn your crew to stand clear of both. In severe weather, the helicopter pilot may instruct you to detach the litter from the hoist cable in order to give him more maneuverability while you load the patient. In other cases, you may have to move the litter from the hoist area to the inside of your vessel to load the patient. The litter must never be moved from the hoist area without first detaching it from the hoist cable.

- **Load patient in litter and strap in. If necessary, reattach litter to hoist cable.**

Place the victim in the litter, making sure his or her arms and legs are well inside. If the litter is provided with straps, use them to strap the victim in the litter securely. It normally is not a good idea to cover the victim with a blanket, as it could become entangled in the hoist mechanism.

- **Signal helicopter to hoist litter with "thumbs up."**

Do not give the helicopter the hoist signal until you are sure that the patient is well secured in the litter and all your crew are clear of the litter, the hoist cable, and the trail line.

• **During hoisting, steady litter to keep it clear of obstructions. Use trail line to steady litter until it is clear of vessel.**

Hoisting the litter with the victim in it is potentially the most dangerous part of the evacuation process, particularly in heavy winds and/or seas. Use all available crew to help steady the litter until it is clear of your vessel, but caution them to watch themselves as well. The last thing you need in this situation is to have one of your healthy crew members fall overboard.

During the hoisting operation, the pilot will try to hold the helicopter as steady as possible to allow the hoist person to bring the litter aboard with an electric winch. In heavy weather it may take the weight of several members of your crew on the trail line to keep the litter steady until it is well clear of any obstructions on your vessel. Once the litter is clear, throw any remaining part of the trail line overboard to leeward, making sure it does not become entangled with any part of your vessel or any of your crew.

CHAPTER SIX

HULL DAMAGE

- Identify location and source of incoming water.

- Be alert to possible discharge of electric current into bilge water.

- Try to stem water flow.

- Check automatic bilge pumps for proper operation.

- If bilge pumps are inoperative or inadequate to handle water flow, engage auxiliary pumps.

- If bilge and auxiliary pumps appear insufficient to handle water flow, send out alerting and/or distress signals.

- Abandon vessel for life raft only as last resort; stay with main vessel for as long as possible.

• **Identify location and source of incoming water.**

A significant quantity of water flowing into your vessel's hull can quickly become a dangerous, even life-threatening, emergency. At the first sign that there has been a serious breach of your hull's integrity, do whatever you must to quickly identify where water is entering your vessel and the nature of the leak with which you are dealing. Speed here is of the essence. If a dangerous amount of water is gushing into your vessel from an inaccessible location—under a berth or below the galley sole, for instance—don't be fastidious about stripping away whatever is blocking your view of the problem. You can repair a few hundred dollars'-worth of damage much more cheaply than you can replace your entire boat—and you can't replace human lives at all.

Other than a collision, the most common sources of significant hull leaks are the failure of through-hull fittings, hoses, keel bolts, underwater exhausts, rudder posts, and stuffing boxes. Check those locations first.

• **Be alert to possible discharge of electric current into bilge water.**

If your vessel has suffered hull damage as the result of a collision, be alert to the possibility that the collision might also have damaged the vessel's electrical system. Water is an excellent, potentially deadly, conductor of electricity. If a live electrical wire has been knocked loose and is discharging current into bilge water, anyone stepping or reaching into that bilge water could sustain a serious, possibly fatal, shock. If any electrical wires have been pulled loose and come into contact with bilge water, or you notice any electrical sparking, shut down the main breakers in your AC and DC electrical panels before exposing yourself to the water in the bilge.

- **Try to stem water flow.**

The action you take to try to stem the flood of water coming into your vessel will depend on the nature of the leak itself. If the problem is a ruptured raw-water intake hose, simply closing the sea cock or gate valve that serves it should solve the immediate problem. If the hose is one that delivers cooling water to your main engine or generator, shut the engine or generator down until you effect repairs, to avoid the danger of burning it out.

Stuffing boxes are designed to weep a minimal amount of water as a lubricant and to insure that they are not too tight, but vibration can cause the packing nuts to work loose and allow a significant amount of water to enter the hull in a short time. Make certain you always have on board a pair of large pliers, a wrench, or a special packing-nut tool big enough to retighten the nuts if they work loose while under way.

All through-hull fittings serving raw-water intakes should be fitted with a sea cock or gate valve, but if you come across one that isn't, you can at least slow the flood of incoming water by wrapping the hose with waterproof tape and/or rags. Every vessel's engine-room should be equipped with several rolls of a product called Syntho-Glass™ resin-impregnated tape. The resin sets up within 30 minutes of being saturated with water and forms a strong, temporary repair. Since it is heat-resistant to 1,100° F, it can even be used on exhaust systems and mufflers. It can be wrapped around a broken hose or balled up and used to plug small openings such as a failed through-hull fitting.

Every through-hull fitting should have a conical wooden plug of appropriate diameter attached to it with a piece of light line. If a through-hull fails and its sea cock or gate valve cannot be closed, simply ram the plug home to stem the flow of water. Shaft glands should also be fitted with wooden

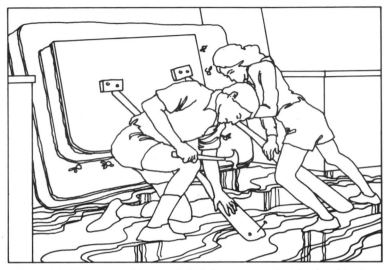

Figure 6.1 If your vessel is severely holed, use any material at hand to stem the flow of water into your vessel and brace it securely in place.

plugs. In 1989 a sailing vessel went down off Bermuda because her prop became entangled in a fishing net and the entire shaft was literally wrenched out of the boat. One life was lost in the accident. Plugs should also be fitted to any rudder post glands that open into the hull.

If the problem is a breach in the hull itself resulting from a collision, stuff the opening from inside the hull with any soft materials you can lay your hands on, such as berth cushions, pillows, or blankets—but never life jackets, you might need them (fig. 6.1). As quickly as possible, reinforce these soft materials with something flat and solid, such as a hatch cover or dinette-table top, and wedge it into place with whatever bracing material comes to hand, such as a dinette-table support, a boat hook, or dinghy oars. If the breach is below your vessel's waterline, you can also reduce the flow of water by covering it on the outside of the hull with a collision mat, a sail, or awning material held in place by ropes. Water pressure outside the hull will help hold it in position. If you are going to try to reach shore with such a rig in place, make certain its top edge is well above your vessel's waterline.

- **Check automatic bilge pumps for proper operation.**

As soon as you have the source of incoming water under a reasonable degree of control, make sure that your vessel's automatic electric bilge pumps are working properly by placing your hand near their water inlets to check for suction. If you don't feel water being sucked into a pump, make certain its inlet is not clogged with debris, that its float valve is not stuck in the "off" position, and that it is receiving proper electrical power.

- **If bilge pumps are inoperative or inadequate to handle water flow, engage auxiliary pumps.**

The best electric bilge pump—or even two or three of them—probably can't handle a serious breach of hull integrity. The electric bilge pumps typically found on vessels under 50 feet are rated at about 1,500 to 2,000 gallons per hour, which translates into only 25 to 33 gallons per minute. Those on vessels over 50 feet may go up to about 3,500 gallons per hour, but that is still less than 60 gallons per minute. A four-inch hole in your hull well below the waterline could easily admit 200 gallons per minute.

You can supplement your vessel's electric bilge pumps with manual bilge pumps, the largest of which can move up to a gallon a stroke. The problem, of course, is that the crew has to operate them, and this is strenuous work. Most people are not able to operate a good-sized manual bilge pump at thirty to forty strokes per minute for more than about ten minutes, so you'll have to set up a rotating schedule.

In a serious emergency, you can remove a significant quantity of water from your vessel by using your main engine and/or the engine powering your electrical generator as an emergency bilge pump. The raw-water pump on a typical 6-cylinder diesel engine, for instance, has a flow rate of about 75 gallons per minute, and one on a 12-cylinder engine pumps up to 140 gallons per minute. Here's the procedure: If the engine is running, turn it off. Close the sea cock or gate valve of the through-hull fitting serving the engine's raw-water intake, disconnect the hose clamps, remove the hose from the through-hull, cover its end with some kind of screening to keep out debris (if nothing else is available, rip the wire out of a port or companionway screen), lay the end of the inlet hose in the bilge, and restart the engine. The end of the inlet hose must be completely covered by bilge water to insure that the engine gets an adequate supply of cooling water. You should also post a crew member at the end of the inlet hose to make certain it does not become clogged and to alert you to the moment when the engine has pumped out enough water so that it is no longer receiving an adequate supply of cooling water.

• **If bilge and auxiliary pumps appear insufficient to handle water flow, send out alerting and/or distress signals.**

The instant you doubt your ability to control the flow of water coming into your vessel's hull, or at least to pump the water overboard faster than it is coming in, broadcast a Pan-Pan urgency message (see page 189 for the correct procedure) over VHF Channel 16 or SSB frequency 2182 kHz to sound an alert that you may need assistance. State the nature of your emergency and the assistance you require. Be sure to include your location by latitude and longitude or relative to well-known landmarks, give a description of your vessel, and note the number of people on board. If you reach the Coast Guard and are within range of one of their helicopters or C-130s, they may be able to air-drop an emergency gasoline-powered bilge pump to you. The instructions for operating it will be on the canister. Don't put off making at least an alerting call, as your batteries could quickly be shorted out by the incoming water.

The moment you become convinced that you are not going to be able to keep your vessel from foundering, broadcast a Mayday distress message (see page 178 for the correct procedure). If you don't get a satisfactory reply to your Mayday, set off visible and possibly audible distress signals. Even if you cannot see any other vessels in your immediate vicinity, fire a red parachute or a meteor flare. It might be spotted by a vessel out of sight over the horizon that will come to investigate. If other vessels are nearby, sound repeated short blasts on your horn, raise and lower your fully extended arms, display your orange distress flag with square and circle, and/or fire an orange smoke flare.

These steps, of course, assume that you are far from shore when your hull's integrity is seriously breached. If you are inshore and can reach land or even a sandbar, simply run your vessel aground. You may do some further damage to your hull and possibly your underwater gear, but at least you will keep your boat from going under.

- **Abandon vessel for life raft only as last resort; stay with main vessel for as long as possible.**

If all else fails, launch your life raft and go through your abandon-ship drill (see pages 11-22). If your vessel doesn't sink completely but is simply awash, stay near it if at all possible to improve your chances of being spotted.

CHAPTER SEVEN

MAN OVERBOARD

- The crew member who sees a person go overboard should immediately and loudly shout, "Man Overboard!," continually keep his or her eyes on the MOB, point emphatically toward the victim, and not assume or accept, or be assigned, any other duties.

- Jettison MOB rig.

- Note compass heading, wind speed, wind direction, and time.

- If under power, reduce throttle and reverse course to reciprocal in as tight a turn as possible. If wind is other than dead astern, make turn to leeward.

- If under sail, reverse course to reciprocal and start engine if you have one.

- Reaccelerate toward MOB, following directions of crew member pointing toward the victim, and approach from downwind to within about ten feet.

CONTINUED

- Shift to reverse to lose all headway, shift to neutral, throw floating line with float attached to MOB, and hoist person aboard amidships.

- If MOB is injured or unconscious, approach to within about ten feet, then dispatch strongest crew member into water to retrieve him or her.

- If assistance of other vessels is required, broadcast Pan-Pan urgency signal, preceded by radiotelephone alarm if possible. Once emergency is over, a Pan-Pan urgency signal broadcast "to all ships" must be canceled.

- The crew member who sees a person go overboard should immediately and loudly shout, "Man Overboard!," continually keep his or her eyes on the MOB, point emphatically toward the victim, and not assume or accept, or be assigned, any other duties.

This reaction must be instantaneous. A crew member who sees someone fall into the water must from that very second keep his or her eyes constantly on the person overboard and not be distracted from doing so for even a second. Under the best of conditions, a human being in the sea can be difficult to spot. In heavy seas or poor visibility, spotting that person can be virtually impossible. Once visual contact is lost, it can be extremely difficult, if not impossible, to reestablish.

The crew member who is keeping watch on the MOB will provide the primary reference for returning to the victim. By emphatically pointing toward the MOB with a fully extended arm, this "spotter" will give the person at the helm vital information as to how to maneuver the vessel to return to the pickup point. With luck, the spotter will be able to remain in full view of the helmsperson as he or she performs this vital task, but keeping the MOB in sight is the spotter's first—indeed only—responsibility. If necessary, another crew member must relay the spotter's directions to the helmsperson.

If several crew members spot the MOB, they likewise should keep their eyes fixed firmly on the victim and point emphatically in his or her direction until the captain orders them to assist in handling the vessel. One crew member, however, must be clearly assigned as a spotter to keep the MOB in sight and point to him or her. This person should be given no other task.

- **Jettison MOB rig.**

Your vessel should be equipped with an MOB rig, which consists of a buoyant, weighted pole at least eight feet long, with its top marked by a large international orange flag and a water-activated strobe light. The rig should also include an attached horseshoe life-ring, a whistle, and a small drogue, and you should be able to launch the entire apparatus in a matter of seconds. If you do not have an MOB rig aboard, throw a life jacket, life ring, or floating cushion overboard the instant you hear the Man Overboard! cry. Your purpose is not only to give the MOB something to cling to, but to provide yourself with a visual reference to guide you to the victim's vicinity. If the person goes overboard at night, in rain, or in fog, and you have a separate water-activated MOB strobe light, throw that as well. Unless the weather is calm, visibility is excellent, and you have the MOB clearly in sight, it's also a good idea to have a crew member jettison anything that floats and is easily visible at about one-minute intervals throughout the rescue process. If you encounter difficulty in immediately locating the MOB, this trail of floating objects will give you information about wind and current conditions and will be invaluable in helping you determine how to conduct your search for the victim most effectively. Some experienced cruisers and offshore racers carry a large magazine or catalog for just this purpose and have a crew member tear out a page, ball it up, and throw it overboard at one minute intervals.

- **Note compass heading, wind speed, wind direction, and time.**

If you lose sight of the MOB and must conduct a search for him or her, the baseline of that search will be your vessel's track or the reciprocal of the course you were running when you first realized that the person had gone over the side.

There is no way you can establish that baseline if you do not know your compass heading, so note it before you make your turn.

If you must conduct a search, you will find yourself calculating current vectors over time to estimate the direction in which the MOB is likely to have drifted and the distance he or she is likely to have been carried. To figure those, you are going to need accurate base references. The time the person went overboard is especially critical. In the tension of a search, time seems to be compressed and you could easily mistake how long the MOB has been in the water and thus miscalculate his or her most likely position.

If at all possible, write these factors down. If that is impractical, tell them to another crew member, with orders to help you remember them in case any of them slip your own mind in the excitement.

- **If under power, reduce throttle and reverse course in as tight a turn as possible. If wind is other than dead astern, make turn to leeward.**

The objective of this maneuver is to get your vessel turned around and headed back toward the MOB as quickly as possible and, starting from a position as closely as possible to the point at which the Man Overboard! alarm was sounded, to sail back toward the MOB on as close as possible to a reciprocal of your original heading.

If you do not reduce speed before making your turn, it can describe an arc of up to several hundred yards, depending on how fast you are going, which will alter your starting point on the reciprocal by the diameter of the turn's arc.

As nearly as possible, you want to spin your vessel on its keel so you begin the reciprocal course as close as possible to the point at which you began to make the turn. In a sailboat operating under power alone or in a single-engine powerboat, reduce throttle, shift to neutral, shift briefly to reverse and give a brief burst of throttle to lose as much headway as possible, reduce throttle, shift back to forward gear, then make your turn tightly. In a twin-screw powerboat, do the same, but leave your windward engine in forward and put your leeward engine in reverse to pivot your vessel in the tightest possible turn.

The reason for turning to leeward if the wind is other than dead downwind is that from the moment of going over the side, the MOB has been floating downwind. By turning your vessel to leeward, you increase your chances of putting yourself on a reciprocal which will intercept the victim. If you turn to windward, you are increasing your vessel's divergence from his or her likely course.

- **If under sail, reverse course to reciprocal and start engine if you have one.**

As with a powerboat, you want to turn around and head back toward the person in the water on a reciprocal of your original heading as quickly and accurately as possible. How you do that most efficiently will depend on your point of sail at the moment you hear the cry Man Overboard! and is discussed below.

Regardless of your point of sail, do not attempt to immediately drop or furl your sails. That maneuver will only take up critical time and can distract your crew from keeping the person in the water in sight. Do, however, start your engine as quickly as is practical, to give yourself increased maneuverability both in returning to and in effecting the recovery of the MOB. Once you have sighted and are sailing back toward the person, it is appropriate to drop or furl your sails, but only if your crew can accomplish the procedure without loosing sight of the victim or otherwise interfering with the rescue effort.

If sailing with the wind on your bow or quarter, fall off and jibe.

Some marine safety texts advise that the moment the helmsperson of a sailing vessel realizes a crew member has gone overboard, he or she should immediately round up to windward in order to stop the boat as quickly as possible. This maneuver is appropriate if the accident occurs during daylight hours when visibility is unobscured, if sea and wind conditions are reasonably calm, if the Man Overboard! alarm is sounded immediately after the person goes over the side, and if the MOB can be kept clearly in sight at all times. It is inappropriate advice, however, when the individual goes overboard in darkness or visibility is sharply reduced by rain or fog, when the wind is blowing over about 20 knots or a considerable sea is running, or when the Man Overboard! alarm is not sounded immediately after the person goes over the side. Under any of those conditions, it is highly likely that the MOB will be lost from sight and the primary task will be in locating him or her. From the moment of going overboard, the MOB has been floating downwind. If you round up to windward, you are increasing your vessel's divergence from his or her likely course. By falling off to leeward and jibing, you increase your chances of putting yourself on a reciprocal course that will intercept the person in the water.

If sailing dead downwind, turn to side opposite that on which main is set, and tack.

In a dead downwind situation, turning to the side opposite that on which the main is set, allows you to return with only one tack to the point at which the MOB went over the side. If you turn to the side on which the main is set, you will have to execute first a jibe, then a tack, to return to your reciprocal course. Having to execute two maneuvers can consume valuable time and distract your crew from keeping the MOB in sight.

- **Reaccelerate toward MOB, following directions of crew member pointing toward the victim, and approach from downwind to within about ten feet.**

If the MOB is obviously conscious and uninjured, one of the easiest methods for getting him or her back on board is to tie a life jacket, life ring, seat cushion or other buoyant object to the end of a line about fifty feet long (a device called a Lifesling™ is designed specifically for this purpose), trail that line off your vessel's stern, then sail slowly around the MOB in decreasing circles until he or she can grab the line. Once the MOB has hold of the line, bring the vessel head-to-wind, pull the MOB to the boat and hoist him or her aboard amidships.

If it is necessary to bring your vessel up to the MOB, approach from the leeward side. Some texts on marine safety advocate approaching the MOB from windward, the idea being that the vessel thus creates a lee in which the MOB can be hauled on board. Again, this may be appropriate in settled conditions of wind and sea. But in winds over about 20 knots or when a considerable sea is running, the practice can be extremely dangerous. Even a sailing vessel of 20 feet or so can easily weigh 5,000 to 6,000 pounds. That much weight being lifted on a six foot sea and slammed down on a person in the water can have disastrous results. By approaching the MOB from downwind, you reduce the likelihood of your vessel being driven down on him or her by wind and current. You also increase your ability to maneuver with less danger of

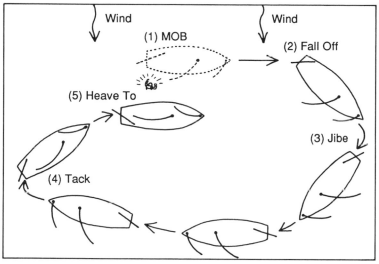

Figure 7.1 To recover a person overboard (1) when sailing to windward: fall off to leeward (2), jibe your vessel's stern through the wind (3), sail back to a point just beyond and to leeward of the person in the water, then tack (4) without releasing your windward jib sheet and turn your rudder to windward. If properly executed, this manuever will leave your vessel hove-to just to leeward of the person in the water (5). Heave a line to the person in the water and bring him or her aboard amidships.

striking the victim with the vessel or its propeller(s). To further reduce the danger of causing injury with the vessel, approach to within about ten feet rather than bringing the vessel right up to the MOB.

If your sails are still hoisted, some forty to fifty feet before you reach the pickup point (depending on the heft of your vessel and wind and current conditions) release the main and jib sheets and luff your sails in order to lose forward way before you reach the MOB.

If your vessel does not have an engine or its engine is inoperable, do not drop or furl your sails as you approach the MOB. Wind and current could drive you away and require you to execute additional maneuvers to reach the person. If your sails are flying, you can achieve the necessary headway simply by hardening up. If you drop or furl sails, you will have to raise or unfurl them to make another approach.

If you find yourself maneuvering an engineless sailing vessel through a MOB pickup in heavy weather, you can greatly increase its stability during the recovery by heaving-to just to leeward of the person in the water (fig. 7.1). To execute the maneuver, approach the MOB from downwind on a tack, but aim your bow far enough to leeward of the victim to allow yourself to tack just beneath him or her. As you come abeam of the MOB, execute a tack. Put your helm over and allow your main to come over as in a normal tack, but do not release your leeward jib sheet from its winch. As your bow passes through the eye of the wind, put you rudder hard over to windward and hold it there. The rudder and sheeted main will be trying to force your vessel to round up, but the backsheeted jib will prevent it. Thus balanced, your vessel will maintain her position relative to the wind and slowly drift to leeward. Have a crew member posted on the bow to heave a line to the MOB as soon as she comes within range.

Another technique for holding a sailing vessel steady while you effect the recovery of a MOB is the "Rod-stop" method developed by sailing expert Rod Stephens. It involves approaching the MOB on a close reach, furling, dowsing or luffing the jib, casting off the main sheet, securing the boom tightly against the leeward shrouds with a line which runs from the end of the boom through a fitting at the bow and back to the cockpit, then flattening the mainsail with a tightly-cinched boom vang. This is a fine technique, provided the vessel is already rigged with a preventer and boom vang. The typical cruising sailboat may well not have such lines in place, and a MOB situation is not the time to try to rig them.

FORMAT FOR TRANSMITTING
Pan-Pan
URGENCY CALL AND MESSAGE

1. "PAN-PAN   PAN-PAN   PAN-PAN"   (properly pronounced PAHN-PAHN).

2. "ALL STATIONS" (or the name of a particular vessel).

3. "THIS IS _____, _____."
   (your boat name)   (your call sign)

4. "WE _____."
   (state nature of your emergency)

5. "WE REQUIRE _____."
   (state type of assistance required or give other
   useful information such as your position, a
   description of your vessel, or the number of
   people on board)

6. "THIS IS _____, _____."
   (your boat name)   (your call sign)

7. "OVER."

Figure 7.2   To summon assistance in a man overboard situation, transmit the Pan-Pan Urgency Call and Message, according to the above format, rather than the Mayday Distress Call and Message.

- **Shift to reverse to lose all headway, shift to neutral, throw floating line with float attached to MOB, and hoist person aboard amidships.**

Shifting your engine to neutral will eliminate the danger of striking the MOB with a rotating propeller, yet it will leave the engine ready should you require it for additional maneuvering. Some marine safety texts advise shutting down the engine completely before attempting to approach the MOB. Again, that is appropriate advice in settled conditions

FORMAT FOR CANCELLING A
Pan-Pan
URGENCY CALL AND MESSAGE
BY A VESSEL

1. "PAN-PAN PAN-PAN PAN-PAN."

2. "HELLO ALL STATIONS, HELLO ALL STATIONS, HELLO ALL STATIONS."

3. "THIS IS_____, _____."
               (your boat name)   (your call sign)

4. "THE TIME IS:_____."
               (state time of transmission by 24-hour clock)

5. "_____, _____."
               (your boat name)   (your call sign)

6. "SEELONCE FEENEE."

7. "_____, _____."
               (your boat name)   (your call sign)

8. "OUT."

Figure 7.3

of wind and sea. If the wind is blowing over about 20 knots or a considerable sea is running, the typical weekend sailor is likely to need the engine to position his vessel properly to effect the MOB rescue.

The use of a floating line (if possible) will reduce the danger of fouling a line in your vessel's prop just when it is most needed for maneuvering. Assuming that the MOB is conscious and able to function, throwing out a line to tow him or her to the vessel is safer than bringing the vessel right up to the person or having another crew member enter the water.

In unsettled weather, amidships will be the most stable part of the vessel and is therefore the safest place to hoist an

MOB aboard. If you attempt to bring the MOB aboard at the bow or the stern, either end could be lifted on a wave and the MOB could be struck by it or trapped beneath it.

- **If MOB is injured or unconscious, approach to within about ten feet, then dispatch strongest crew member into water to retrieve him or her.**

Entering the water to rescue an injured or unconscious person can be dangerous and arduous, and the assignment should be given to your strongest crew member. Allow no one to enter the water without being attached to the vessel by a safety line, as that person could be swept away from the vessel by wind and current, which would merely compound your problems. The rescuer should remove his or her shoes and wear a life jacket, both for self-protection and to provide additional buoyancy during the recovery procedure.

- **If assistance of other vessels is required, broadcast Pan-Pan urgency signal, preceded by radiotelephone alarm if possible. Once emergency is over, a Pan- Pan urgency signal broadcast "to all ships" must be canceled.**

The proper signal to use if you require the assistance of other vessels to locate or recover an MOB is the Pan-Pan urgency signal rather than the Mayday distress signal. The proper format for transmitting it will be found in fig. 7.2. Precede the Pan-Pan urgency signal with the radiotelephone alarm signal only in an MOB situation and only if you feel you cannot obtain the required assistance without it.

In crowded conditions such as a yacht race, if you will be able to retrieve the MOB yourself but may have to violate the normal rules of the road to do so, use the Pan-Pan urgency signal to alert other vessels in your vicinity to your intentions and instruct them to stand clear.

The Pan-Pan signal can be directed toward one or more specific vessels or to "all ships." Once the emergency has passed, you are not required to cancel a Pan-Pan urgency signal addressed to one or more specific vessels. If you broadcast a Pan-Pan urgency signal "to all ships," however, once the emergency is ended you must cancel it, using the format in fig. 7.3.

Tips On Conducting an MOB Search

If anyone on your boat sees a fellow crew member go overboard during daylight hours and the visibility is good, recovering the person using the above procedure is relatively simple.

But if no one sees the MOB go over the side, or you lose sight of him or her, here are some tips for conducting a search which should improve your chances of a successful recovery:

- As soon as the MOB alarm is sounded, note the time and your present speed and heading, then stop your vessel.
- If no one saw the MOB go over the side, attempt to establish the amount of time that has elapsed since the person was last seen on board.
- Plot your vessel's present position on your chart and label it as FIX. If your vessel's track (i.e., recent course) is not already charted, plot it as a reciprocal of your present heading.†
- From the time elapsed since the last sighting of the MOB and your vessel's speed during that time, plot the most remote point along your vessel's track at which the MOB

---

† To compute a reciprocal course from a present course of greater than 180 degrees, subtract 180 degrees. If your present course is less than 180 degrees, add 180 degrees.

is likely to have gone over the side. Label that point as MOB 0.

- A person in the water presents so little surface to the wind that wind speed and direction can be virtually discounted as factors in determining the MOB's likely speed and direction of drift. Because two-thirds to three-fourths of the MOB's bulk is in the water, he or she will be affected far more by current. Determine the speed of any current that is running and establish the direction in which it is setting.‡ Plot the direction of set as a line through the point you have labeled MOB 0 and note its estimated speed.

---

‡ The prudent mariner will always be aware of the speed and direction of set of any current that is affecting his or her vessel. If you are not already aware of those factors when the Man Overboard! alarm is sounded and cannot determine them from your navigational instruments (such as a loran unit), here is how to quickly get a basic estimate: To estimate the current's speed, lay your vessel directly head-to-wind and reduce power to the minimum required to maintain steerage. Note the position of your watch's second hand and, at your mark, have a crew member at the point of your bow toss overboard a half-full gallon milk jug or other similar container that can be sealed. Note the number of seconds (T) it takes the jug to float from bow to stern. Divide your vessel's length by T and multiply the result by .6, which will give you the current's approximate speed in knots.

To determine the approximate direction of the current's set, observe the angle at which the jug floats away from your vessel with a hand-bearing compass. If the jug drifts dead downwind, you can use the wind's angle as the current's direction of set. If the angle of the jug's drift differs significantly from the angle of the wind, you know that a strong current is running whose direction of set is not coincident with the wind angle. In that case, disregard wind angle and use the current's direction of set in your calculations.

- Based on the elapsed time since the MOB was last seen and the speed and set of the current, plot the MOB's estimated present position along the line of the current's set and label it MOB 1.

- Plot a course from FIX to MOB 1 as the course you will steer and post lookouts at your vessel's highest point. Measure the distance from FIX to MOB 1 and calculate the time it will take you to get there based on your vessel's speed alone. Remember that during this run, your vessel will be affected by the same current set and drift that is effecting the MOB. Factor the current's effects into your vessel's speed and heading and label the resulting position as V 1.

- If your reaction was instantaneous and your figures are precisely correct, V 1 and MOB 2 will coincide. Regardless of the point along your vessel's track where the MOB actually went over the side, he or she theoretically will have drifted right onto your course. Since it is unlikely that your reaction was instantaneous or that your figures were exact, the victim could be to either side of your course, but at least you will have determined a line of position along which to conduct your search.

- Once you have worked out the MOB's estimated present position and the direction and speed he or she is likely to drift, use the Pan-Pan urgency signal to enlist the aid of any other vessels that might be in that vicinity or along the person's line of drift.

CHAPTER EIGHT

MEDICAL EMERGENCIES

- Conduct rapid assessment of victim to identify primary medical emergency and to determine whether your intervention is required.

- Attend to ABCs of emergency medical-care first: Airway, Breathing, and Circulation.

- Once victim's airway, breathing, and circulation are stable, attend to specific medical emergencies as recommended on the following pages.

Note: Except where otherwise specified, the recommendations in this chapter assume that the victim is an adult or a well-developed child about eight years old. For infants and children less than eight years old, the procedures are essentially the same, but the frequency with which procedures are executed and the force exerted by the rescuer may vary considerably. If you are likely to have infants or children under eight aboard your vessel frequently, you should obtain specialized training for dealing with any medical emergencies they might experience.

- Conduct rapid assessment of victim to identify primary medical emergency and to determine whether your intervention is required.

The injury or difficulty you may notice first is not necessarily the victim's most serious or the one with which you should attempt to deal first. For example: A crew member slips on your vessel's foredeck. You rush to the victim and note an obvious broken arm and a severe gash on the forearm. Before you attempt to treat the broken arm or the wound, you should check to make certain that there is not a far graver difficulty, such as an injury to the spinal column. In this situation, hasty action on your part before you have determined the primary medical emergency could result in an even more serious injury, or possibly even death.

If the victim is conscious, ask, "Are you OK?" As detailed below, the response—or lack of a response—will tell you much about the victim's condition. Ask next, "What happened?" Again, the response will help direct your attention towards the primary emergency.

If the victim does not respond to your questions or is unconscious:

1. CHECK RESPIRATION: Within seconds after being deprived of oxygen, the heart begins to develop dangerous irregular beats. If the brain is deprived of oxygen for as little as four to six minutes, irreversible damage is possible; after six minutes, irreversible damage is highly likely; after ten minutes, it is virtually certain, unless the victim's internal body temperature has been drastically reduced. For those reasons, checking the victim for adequate respiration is your first responsibility.

   If the victim is not obviously inhaling and exhaling independently, put your ear to his or her lips to listen for the passage of air into and out of the lungs. Try to feel breath on your cheek. Look for chest movement. If the person is heavily clothed in a sweater or foul-weather suit, rest your hand lightly on the upper abdomen to feel for movement. A conscious victim grabbing his or her throat or struggling for breath, or a wheezing noise in the breathing of an unconscious victim, indicates an obstruction in the AIRWAY. The absence of breathing may indicate AIRWAY obstruction, RESPIRATORY FAILURE, or HEART ATTACK. A conscious victim who complains of severe chest pain may be suffering ANGINA or be in the early stage of a HEART ATTACK.

2. CHECK CIRCULATION: Feel for the presence of a pulse, preferably at one of the carotid arteries in the victim's neck, since a pulse here is more pronounced than one in the wrist. To locate a carotid artery, place an index and middle finger on the victim's Adam's apple, then slide them to one side into the groove between the Adam's apple and the neck muscle. Check for the presence of a pulse in only one carotid artery at a time, and exert only light pressure; heavy pressure could restrict the flow of blood to the victim's brain.

In checking the victim's circulation, you are primarily concerned with the presence or absence of a pulse. You will be able to tell little about its strength or regularity unless you have some medical training and happen to have a stethoscope and blood pressure cuff available. If you are wearing a watch with a sweep second hand, however, count the pulse for 15 seconds. In a normal, healthy adult, you should count between 15 and 20 beats. The absence of a pulse indicates that the victim has already gone into serious SHOCK or CARDIAC ARREST.

3. CHECK SKIN TEMPERATURE AND MOISTURE: Cool, clammy skin may indicate such conditions as SHOCK, HEAT EXHAUSTION, or INSULIN SHOCK. Hot, dry skin may indicate such conditions as HEAT STROKE and DIABETIC COMA. Flushed skin, swollen welts over large areas of the body, or swelling of the face and lips may indicate ANAPHYLAXIS.

4. CHECK SKIN COLOR: Reddened skin may indicate HEAT STROKE. Pale, white skin indicates such conditions as SHOCK or INSULIN SHOCK. Bluish skin may indicate an obstruction of the victim's AIRWAY, RESPIRATORY FAILURE, or CARDIAC ARREST.

5. CHECK EYE PUPILS: Significant differences in the size of the two pupils can indicate HEAD INJURY. Significant dilation of both pupils may indicate CARDIAC ARREST.

6. CHECK MENTAL ALERTNESS: Significant disorientation may indicate a HEAD INJURY. A victim who is knocked unconscious in an accident, rouses to near normal alertness, then later lapses into unconsciousness again could be suffering from INTERNAL BLEEDING in the head.

7. CHECK MOBILITY: In a conscious victim, total inability to move usually indicates a SPINAL INJURY in the vicinity of the neck. The ability of a conscious victim to move his or her arms but not legs may indicate a SPINAL INJURY below the neck.

Deciding When to Provide Assistance

After you have determined the victim's primary medical emergency but before you do anything, make certain your intervention is truly necessary and warranted. The human body is a remarkable mechanism which often has the capacity to care for itself if simply left alone. Deciding whether and when to intervene is one of the toughest areas of providing emergency medical assistance, especially when professional medical care is a long way off.

IMMEDIATE INTERVENTION is appropriate in three medical emergencies:
1. When the victim is NOT BREATHING at all;
2. When the victim has NO PULSE;
3. When the victim is BLEEDING PROFUSELY from an open wound.

NO IMMEDIATE ACTION on your part other than preventing further injury is appropriate if:
1. You suspect that the victim has suffered a SPINAL INJURY;
2. A conscious victim who can talk or make noise is choking on a foreign body (the victim may well expel it through his or her own exertions);
3. The victim is suffering a CONVULSION or SEIZURE.

WAIT AND SEE is the appropriate attitude if:
1. A victim is conscious but breathing weakly or gasping for breath;
2. The victim has a weak or racing pulse;
3. The victim is unconscious but breathing independently and has a pulse.

In these situations, avoid the "hero syndrome" of rushing to provide assistance that may not be necessary and could actually do more harm than good. Instead, watch the victim carefully, see if a condition develops that warrants your intervention, and call for help.

• Attend to ABCs of emergency medical-care first: Airway, Breathing, and Circulation.

Airway

The victim's airway can be blocked by a foreign object or, especially if unconscious and lying on his or her back, by the soft tissues of the person's own throat and tongue.

If a conscious victim is choking and you suspect that the airway is blocked by a foreign object, do not immediately attempt to assist the person if any air is passing in and out of the lungs. Give the victim time to dislodge the obstruction independently. Only if he or she ceases to pass any air in and out of the lungs should you attempt to help the victim expel the obstruction by employing the Heimlich maneuver: If the victim is standing, get behind him or her and wrap your arms around the person's torso just above the waist (fig. 8.1). Grasp one fist with the other hand and place the thumb side of the fist half way between the victim's belly button and the arch of the ribs where they divide at the lower end of the breastbone. With the help of your other hand, thrust your fist into his abdomen with a sharp, decisive, upward squeeze. If the maneuver does not immediately dislodge the object, repeat your efforts until the object is expelled or the victim loses consciousness.

Choking often causes the muscles in the victim's throat to go into spasm, thereby trapping the object and preventing the passage of air in and out of the lungs. Once the victim looses

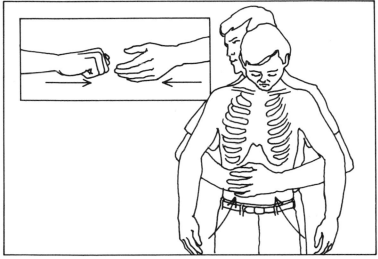

Figure 8.1 To perform the Heimlich maneuver on a standing victim, get behind the person and wrap your arms around his or her torso just above the waist. Grasp one fist with the other hand and place the thumb side of the fist half way between the victim's belly button and the arch of the ribs. Thrust your fist into the abdomen with a sharp, decisive upward squeeze.

consciousness, the spasm often ceases, the object may be released, and the victim may resume normal breathing. If a choking victim lapses into unconsciousness, assist the person gently to the sole or deck, lay the victim flat on his or her back and clear the airway. Never attempt to clear a victim's airway by lifting up on his or her neck. If the victim has suffered a spinal injury in the vicinity of the neck, exerting pressure in that area could inflict severe damage or death. Instead, use the CHIN-LIFT/HEAD-TILT method (fig. 8.2):

Place one hand on the victim's forehead. Place two fingers of the other hand under the point of the victim's jaw. Simultaneously tilt the victim's head backward by pressing on the forehead with one hand while you lift the jaw upward

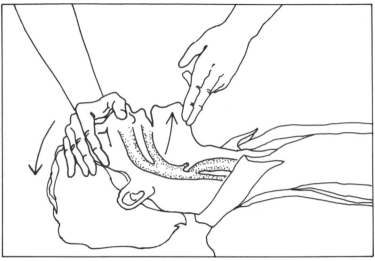

Figure 8.2 To use the chin-lift/head-tilt method to clear a victim's airway: Place one hand on the victim's forehead; place two fingers on the other hand under the front edge of the victim's jaw; then simultaneously tilt the victim's head back by pressing the forehead backward with one hand while you lift the jaw upward with the fingers of the other.

with the fingers of the other. This maneuver will bring the tongue forward and clear it from the airway. Check the victim's RESPIRATION. Often simply clearing the victim's airway will allow air to flow in and out of the lungs and expel the foreign object.

If the victim is still not breathing and his or her mouth is not already open, open it using the CROSS-FINGER technique: cross one index finger over the thumb of the same hand. Place the tip of your thumb on the bottom of the victim's upper teeth and the tip of your index finger on the top of the lower teeth, then force them apart. Holding the mouth open in this fashion, use the forefinger of the other hand to sweep the inside of the victim's mouth and attempt to locate the foreign body and remove it.

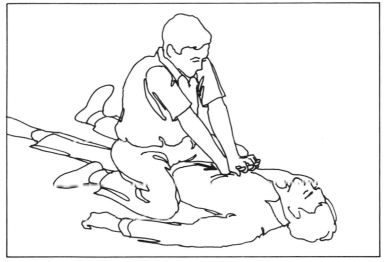

Figure 8.3 To execute the Heimlich maneuver on a prone victim: Straddle the victim's hips; place the heel of one hand against the victim's abdomen halfway between the belly button and the arch of the ribs; point the fingers of that hand toward the victim's head; place your second hand on top of the first; then thrust inward and upward with a sharp, decisive motion.

If you are unable to locate the foreign body, straddle the victim's hips (fig. 8.3). Place the heel of one hand against the victim's abdomen halfway between the belly button and the arch of the ribs where they divide at the lower end of the breastbone. Point the fingers of that hand towards the victim's head. Place your second hand on top of the first. Thrust inward and upward towards the victim's head with a sharp, decisive motion. If the maneuver does not immediately dislodge the object, repeat it six to ten times. Employing the Heimlich maneuver in this way on an unconscious victim who is lying on his or her back may dislodge the foreign body from the person's airway but not expel it from the mouth. If the object is not expelled from the mouth, it may fall to the back of the throat and continue to obstruct the victim's breathing. In this case, open the airway as described above, then see if you can locate the obstruction with a finger sweep and remove it.

Breathing

If an unconscious victim is not breathing after his or her airway has been opened, administer artificial ventilation using MOUTH-TO-MOUTH VENTILATION (fig. 8.4):

Use the CHIN-LIFT/HEAD TILT method to clear the victim's airway. Keep the head tilted back by continuing to exert pressure on the forehead with the heel of one hand. Use

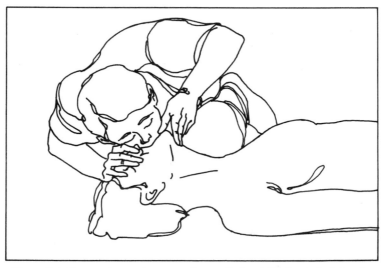

Figure 8.4 To execute mouth-to-mouth ventilation: Tilt the victim's head back by exerting pressure on his or her forehead with the heel of one hand. Use the thumb and forefinger of that same hand to pinch the fleshy tips of the victim's nostrils together. Use the thumb of your other hand to pull down on the victim's chin to keep the mouth open. Open your mouth wide, as if your were preparing to take a big bite out of an apple. Take a deep breath, place your mouth completely over the victim's mouth, and exhale deeply.

the thumb and forefinger of that same hand to pinch the fleshy tips of the victim's nostrils together. Use the thumb of the other hand to pull down on the victim's chin to keep his or her mouth open. Open your mouth wide as if you were preparing to take a big bite out of an apple. Take a deep breath, place your mouth completely over the victim's mouth, and exhale deeply. Out of the corner of your eye, if you exhale hard enough, you should be able to see the victim's chest rise. After exhaling, remove your mouth to allow the chest to fall. Keep your ear near the victim's mouth to listen for breathing, try to feel the breath on your cheek, and watch the chest for signs of movement. If necessary, release the hand holding the chin and place it on the victim's upper abdomen to feel for movement. If the victim is not breathing independently, cover his or her mouth completely with your own and exhale into it a second time hard enough to make the victim's chest expand. You should complete these two breaths in three to five seconds.

If the victim is not breathing independently after your second exhalation, release the hand holding the chin and use it to check the pulse in the carotid artery (see page 101 under CHECK CIRCULATION). If you detect a pulse, continue mouth-to-mouth ventilation at the rate of one exhalation about every five seconds, each exhalation lasting around 1.5 seconds, until the victim is breathing independently.

Circulation

If you do not detect a pulse in the carotid artery, the victim may be suffering CARDIAC ARREST and you must immediately begin to administer CHEST COMPRESSIONS.

If the victim is not already lying on his or her back on a hard, flat surface, move the person to such a position as quickly as possible.

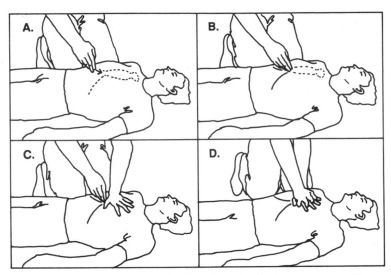

Figure 8.5 To locate the proper hand position for chest compressions: Place the middle finger of your hand that is nearest the victim's feet as high as possible into the arch of his or her ribs (A); lay the forefinger of that hand immediately adjacent to the middle finger (B); place the heel of your other hand on the victim's breastbone immediately adjacent to your forefinger (C); release your hand nearest the victim's feet, place it exactly on top of your other hand, interlock your fingers, and raise them slightly so that you are exerting pressure on the victim's breastbone with the heel of your lower hand only (D).

Kneel next to the victim's chest with your knees slightly apart. One of the most important phases of administering chest compressions is placing your hands in the proper position. Improper hand-placement can result in ineffective compressions, broken ribs or damage to the victim's internal organs. To locate the proper hand-position (fig. 8.5): Place the middle finger of your hand which is nearest the victim's feet as high as possible into the arch where the victim's ribs divide at the breastbone. Lay the forefinger of that hand immediately next to to the middle finger. Place the heel of

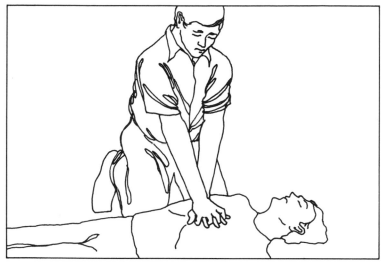

Figure 8.6 To execute chest compressions: Put your hands in position, lock your elbows, and lean forward, rising slightly so your shoulders are directly over the victim's chest and you are exerting pressure directly downward; after depressing the victim's chest 1 1/2 to 2 inches, release pressure just enough to allow the victim's chest to return to its original position.

your other hand on the victim's breastbone, immediately next to to your forefinger. Release your hand nearest the victim's feet, place it exactly on top of your other hand, interlock your fingers, and raise them slightly so that your are exerting pressure on the victim's breastbone with the heel of your lower hand only.

To execute CHEST COMPRESSIONS (fig. 8.6): Lock your elbows and lean forward, rising slightly so that your shoulders are directly over the victim's chest and you are exerting pressure directly downward. After depressing the victim's chest 1 1/2 to 2 inches, release pressure just far enough to allow the victim's chest to return to its original position. Your hands should not bounce off the victim's chest.

Repeat this procedure until you have delivered 15 chest compressions evenly and rhythmically. The process should take about ten seconds.

After 15 chest compressions, quickly shift back to the MOUTH-TO-MOUTH VENTILATION position described on pages 108-109 and check the victim's breathing. If the victim is not breathing independently, deliver two full exhalations into his or her lungs, each exhalation lasting about 1.5 seconds. Allow the victim's chest to fall between breaths.

After two exhalations, return to your chest-compression position, place your hands properly, as described above, and deliver another 15 chest compressions evenly and rhythmically over the next ten to eleven seconds. This combination of mouth-to-mouth ventilation and chest compressions is generally referred to as CARDIO-PULMONARY RESUSCITATION, or CPR. You should always begin and end CPR with mouth-to-mouth ventilation. Maintain this ratio of 15 chest compressions to two mouth-to-mouth ventilations until the victim is breathing independently, or you are relieved by professional medical assistance or another rescuer, or you are exhausted.

If, in addition to administering CPR, you are the only person aboard your vessel who can call for help, the best time to do so is after you have performed four cycles of 15 compressions and two mouth-to-mouth ventilations each. By that time, you should have forced enough air into the victim's lungs and circulated enough oxygenated blood through his or her vital organs with chest compressions to give you a minute and a half to two minutes to try to summon help. Broadcast a Mayday call on VHF Channel 16 or Single Sideband frequency 2182. If you do not get an immediate response, return to the victim and resume CPR, beginning with two exhalations of mouth-to-mouth ventilation.

(CPR conducted by two rescuers with one performing the mouth-to-mouth ventilation and the other performing the chest compressions, requires precise coordination and should not be attempted unless both rescuers are well trained in the procedure. If you have initiated CPR and another individual offers to help, at first continue the CPR by yourself and send the other person to summon help.)

- Once airway, breathing, and circulation are stable, attend to other medical emergencies as recommended below.

Severe Bleeding

EXTERNAL BLEEDING: Apply direct pressure to an open wound by putting your hand over it and pressing firmly and steadily. As soon as possible, put a sterile dressing between your hand and the wound. Once the bleeding stops or slows significantly, apply a compression bandage to the wound: Leave the sterile dressing in place and position the center of a long strip of cloth over it. Maintain a steady pull on the cloth strip as you wrap both ends of it around the body part that has been wounded, then tie a knot directly over the sterile dressing, maintaining pressure.

If possible, elevate the wound above the level of the victim's heart to further retard the flow of blood.

If bleeding continues profusely, restrict the blood flow at the primary artery serving the affected area by pressing the artery against a bone at a pressure point (fig. 8.7).

You should apply a tourniquet only in extreme cases and when all other techniques have failed to stop the bleeding. If applied, a tourniquet (which is practical only if the wound is in an extremity) should not be so tight that it completely cuts off the blood supply from the remainder of the extremity. If the remainder of the extremity beyond the wound begins to turn blue, the tourniquet is too tight. Ease its pressure slowly and gradually. Once you have a tourniquet properly applied, do not loosen or remove it. The sudden loss of blood from the heart could throw the victim into severe SHOCK.

Where blood loss is substantial, treat the victim for SHOCK, as detailed on pages 115-117.

INTERNAL BLEEDING: An individual who suffers a major blow to the abdomen which injures the spleen, a victim who suffers a fracture of the ribs or a large bone, or a person who suffers from a bleeding ulcer, can lose a life-threatening amount of blood with little or no external signs of the bleeding.

Bleeding, however slight, from the rectum, nonmenstrual

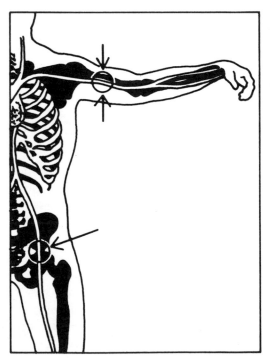

Figure 8.7 The primary pressure points for controlling severe bleeding in an arm or leg are located on the inside of the upper arm and on the inside of the groin.

bleeding from the vagina, blood in the victim's urine or stool, or the coughing or spitting up of blood should lead you to suspect internal bleeding. Bleeding from the nose, mouth, or ears can also indicate internal bleeding, especially if it is not obviously the result of a cut inside the mouth or recent scuba-diving activity.

If the victim is suffering from severe internal bleeding, these signs often will be accompanied by symptoms of shock, such as a weak, rapid pulse; cold, moist skin; dull eyes with pupils that are slow to respond to light; excessive thirst; nausea; vomiting; anxiety; and a marked feeling of depression. The stomach of a person suffering from a lacerated spleen may become tender and swollen.

If the internal bleeding is the result of a large broken bone in the arm or leg, applying a splint will help slow the bleeding. Aside from applying a splint and treating the victim for SHOCK, there is virtually nothing you can do to treat severe internal bleeding without advanced medical training and sophisticated equipment. The victim's condition may well be life-threatening. You should call for help and, if you cannot transport the victim to medical assistance within half an hour, request helicopter evacuation.

Shock

Shock is a collapse of the cardiovascular system in which the flow of blood, which carries oxygen to the body's vital organs, slows and eventually ceases (death). After even a few minutes without an adequate flow of oxygenated blood, the cells of certain organs, primarily the brain and the heart, die and cannot be regenerated.

Shock can be brought on by a number of causes, such as severe blood or fluid loss due to a large open wound, burn, or internal bleeding; damage to the spinal cord that disrupts its control of the nervous system; the dilation of blood vessels in reaction to excessive heat; and failure of the heart to pump effectively.

The signs of shock may include cold, clammy skin; profuse sweating; a pale skin color and, in the advanced stages of shock, a bluish color to the lips; shallow, labored gasping or rapid breathing; a weak, rapid pulse; extreme thirst; nausea; or vomiting.

To treat for shock, clear and maintain the victim's AIRWAY. Lay the victim on his or her back and cover with blankets or clothing to keep warm, but do not employ artificial sources of heat, such as heating pads, electric blankets, or hot-water bottles, and do not allow the victim to become overheated. If available, administer oxygen. If the victim exhibits no signs of head, neck, or back injuries or is not experiencing convulsions, seizures, or respiratory distress; elevate his or her feet eight to twelve inches higher than the head. Elevating the feet places the weight of the internal organs on the diaphragm, which could cause breathing problems, so watch the victim carefully for signs of labored breathing and lower the feet if it occurs.

A victim of shock is likely to complain of intense thirst. If medical help is less than two hours away, do not give fluids but allow the person to suck on a piece of moistened gauze or cloth. If medical assistance is more than two hours away, give fluids only if the victim is conscious and shows no signs of brain, abdominal, or respiratory injury and is not convulsing. The best fluid to administer is a mixture of one level teaspoon of salt and one-half level teaspoon of baking soda dissolved in a quart of tepid water. For adults, give not more than one ounce every 15 minutes; for children one to twelve years old, give half that amount; for infants to one year old, give one quarter that amount. Never give a victim of shock any type of alcohol.

ANAPHYLAXIS, a type of shock that can be caused by severe allergic reaction, ingestion of a food or medicine to which the victim is allergic, and by stings from insects and hazardous marine life, is discussed on pages 131-132, under POISONING.

Open Wounds

If a wound is bleeding severely, attempt to staunch the flow of blood as discussed on pages 113-114, then treat the victim for SHOCK. If a severe wound is in one of the victim's extremities, apply a splint, which will help to control the bleeding, help to prevent bleeding from resuming if the victim must be moved or transported, and help to relieve the victim's pain.

If an open wound involves a flap of skin that has been partially torn from the body, attempt to maintain blood circulation in the flap by realigning it to its original position, making certain that the portion that remains attached is not twisted or kinked. Apply a dry, sterile dressing and a compression bandage. If the injury involves a flap of skin or a portion of an extremity that has been entirely torn from the victim's body, wrap it in sterile gauze, place it in a plastic bag, and keep it in a cool place until you can transport it and the victim to professional medical assistance. Do not allow the flap or portion of the extremity to freeze.

An open wound that exposes internal organs in the abdomen must be kept moist. Cover or wrap the wound with a moistened sterile dressing, cover the dressing with material that is impermeable to air, such as plastic food-wrap or aluminum foil, then secure the impermeable material in place with tape on three sides only.

In the case of a sucking chest wound where air is escaping from the victim's lung, cover the wound with a dry, sterile dressing, shut off the escaping air by wrapping the victim's chest with plastic kitchen wrap or other air-impervious dressing, then secure the impermeable material in place with tape on three sides only.

If an open wound is not bleeding profusely, remove foreign particles with gauze, cleanse the wound with soap and water, and blot it dry. If medical attention will be available within six hours, apply a dry, sterile dressing and a bandage. If medical attention will not be available within six hours, saturate the wound with an antiseptic solution before applying the sterile bandage. One exception to this rule is cuts from coral, which should be cleaned as above but left uncovered and open to the air. Contrary to some folk beliefs, salt water is not a curative, but contains all sorts of contaminants. Therefore, open cuts should not be reimmersed in salt water until they are well healed.

Puncture Wounds

Do not remove an object protruding from a puncture wound if its removal is likely to induce severe bleeding. Leave the object in place, saturate the entry- and, if necessary, the exit-wound with antiseptic solution, cover the wound(s) with a dry, sterile dressing, and bandage the object securely in place. If the injury is severe, treat the victim for SHOCK (pages 115-117).

If you remove the object, cleanse the entry- and, if necessary, the exit-wound with soap and water, saturate the wound(s) with antiseptic solution, then apply a dry, sterile dressing and bandage. If the injury is severe, treat the victim for SHOCK.

A fishhook that has penetrated the skin far enough to bury its barb is best left in place if medical assistance will be available within approximately eight hours. If it will be much longer than eight hours before the victim can reach medical assistance, the possibility of a serious infection in the bloodstream dictates that the hook should be removed. First determine how far the barb has penetrated below the skin surface. If it is less than about a quarter of an inch, clean the area around the hook's entry into the skin with soap and water, saturate it with antiseptic solution, and make a small incision with a razor blade or sharp knife that has been sterilized by being dipped in alcohol or held over a flame, then allowed to cool. Make a small incision behind the barb to expose its tip, grasp the shank of the hook with a pair of needle-nose pliers, and back the hook out. If the barb has penetrated much more than a quarter of an inch beneath the surface of the skin, the best course is to force the point of the hook on through the flesh until the barb emerges, clip it off with wire cutters, then grasp the shank of the hook with a pair of needle-nose pliers and back the remainder of the hook out. In either case, after removing the hook, soak the area liberally with antiseptic solution and massage the area to encourage the solution to penetrate into the wound as deeply as possible. Blot the wound dry and cover it with a sterile dressing and bandage. If available, administer a general antibiotic such as penicillin. As soon as possible, consult a doctor regarding the advisability of the victim receiving a tetanus booster shot.

Fractures and Dislocations

Do not attempt to set a fracture or force a dislocated bone back into its socket. Immobilize the affected area with a splint constructed of any material that is close to hand, such as a dinghy oar, a rolled newspaper or magazine, or even a pillow. If the skin in the vicinity of the fracture is broken, treat it as an OPEN WOUND with an antiseptic sterile dress (pages 117-

118), control any SEVERE BLEEDING (pages 113-114), and treat the victim for SHOCK (pages115-117).

If you suspect a SPINAL INJURY, do not move the victim. Immobilize him or her, especially the head and neck, with at-hand materials such as pillows, settee cushions, or boat cushions placed on each side of the head, and call for medical assistance immediately.

Chest Pain

A victim who complains of tightness or a severe pain in the chest may be suffering from a lack of oxygen to the heart muscle. If the tightness or pain follows a period of exertion, emotional stress, or even a big meal, it may be ANGINA, which is due to a constriction of the vessels that deliver blood to the heart. The pain of angina most commonly begins under the breastbone and may spread to the left arm, the jaw, and the upper region of the abdomen. An attack of angina in itself is not life-threatening and does not result in permanent damage to the heart. If it is the result of exertion or stress, it can often be relieved simply by allowing the victim to rest in a cool, calm location, during which the supply of oxygen gradually equals the heart muscle's oxygen requirement. Many individuals who suffer occasional attacks of angina carry with them a small bottle of nitroglycerin tablets, which rapidly dilate blood vessels, thus dramatically increasing the flow of oxygenated blood. If nitroglycerin is available, have the victim place one tablet beneath his or her tongue and allow it to dissolve. If the pain persists, administer additional nitroglycerin tablets at the rate of about one every three to five minutes. If the pain is indeed angina, it should subside within six to eight minutes. Due to nitroglycerin's rapid dilation of blood vessels, the victim may be left with a mild or even a severe headache, which should ease after a half-hour or so of quiet rest.

If an individual experiences tightness or severe pain in the chest that does not follow a period of exertion or stress, is not relieved by nitroglycerin, or lasts more than ten to fifteen minutes, it may be the result of a far more serious situation—a blood clot blocking the main artery that delivers blood to the heart muscle—a heart attack. If the blockage is complete, the heart can immediately develop an irregular beat or cease to beat at all, and death can be virtually instantaneous. If the blockage is not complete but is substantial, death or serious damage to the heart muscle may result within minutes of the onset of the attack.

If an individual aboard your vessel complains of tightness in the chest or severe chest pain that meets the above description, your response may literally be the difference between the person's life and death:

First, remain calm and deal with the victim in a reassuring manner. Agitating or alarming an ill person can cause the situation to deteriorate quickly.

Allow the victim to sit in a cool, quiet location and observe the person to see if the pain passes. Make certain he or she is breathing easily and regularly. If nitroglycerin is available, have the victim place one tablet under his or her tongue about every three to five minutes. If the pain increases rather than decreases and persists for more than about fifteen minutes, call for help. If you will not be able to transport the victim to professional medical assistance within thirty minutes, request emergency helicopter evacuation.

If a person experiences difficulty in breathing, or stops breathing, loses his or her pulse, his or her eyes roll back in the head, or a seizure occurs, that person may well be experiencing serious and life-threatening CARDIAC ARREST.

As quickly as possible, lay the victim on his or her back on a hard surface, make certain the AIRWAY is clear, assist in BREATHING with two full MOUTH-TO-MOUTH VENTI-

LATIONS and check his or her pulse. If you do not detect a pulse, assist the individual's CIRCULATION with CHEST COMPRESSIONS as detailed on page 111. Call for help as soon as possible and request emergency evacuation.

Drowning Accidents

Enter the water to rescue a drowning victim only as a last resort, as by doing so you risk becoming a drowning victim yourself. The rule is, "THROW, TOW, ROW, and only then, GO." First, THROW the victim a floating object, such as a life jacket, a life ring, or a buoyant cushion. If that is impractical, throw or push an object such as a rope or dinghy oar out to the victim and TOW him to safety. If the distance is too great, attempt to ROW out to the victim in a dinghy or even on a surf board, a sail board, or any other object that will float. Only if all these methods are impractical should you enter the water and attempt a rescue yourself. Even then, be alert to the probability that the person will be panicky and may well attempt to grab hold of you and could pull you down with him or her. If at all possible, approach from behind and try to get the person to calm down, then wrap your arm over his or her shoulder and grasp with your hand below the armpit to tow the person to safety on his or her back.

Remove the victim from the water, roll onto side so water drains from the mouth, and then CHECK his or her AIRWAY. In a drowning incident, the victim's larynx often involuntarily constricts in a spasm in an attempt to keep water from entering the lungs. The spasm will normally relax as soon as the victim is removed from the water. If not, attempt to restore the victim's BREATHING by administering two exhalations of MOUTH-TO-MOUTH VENTILATION (pages 108-109). Check the victim's CIRCULATION by taking the pulse at the carotid artery (page101). If no pulse is felt, execute CHEST COMPRESSIONS (page 111). Alternate 15 chest compressions with two mouth-to-mouth ventilations until the victim is breathing independently, or you are relieved by trained medical assistance or another rescuer, or you are exhausted.

If, in addition to administering CPR, you are the only person aboard your vessel who can call for help, the best time to do so is after you have performed four cycles of 15 compressions and two mouth-to-mouth ventilations each. As noted on page 112 under CIRCULATION, by that time you should have forced enough air into the victim's lungs and compressed the heart enough to give you a minute and a half to two minutes to try to summon help.

Scuba-Diving Accidents

The most serious scuba-diving accidents are those related to ascending from a dive to the surface too rapidly or to failing to breath normally during an ascent.

As a scuba diver descends into the water, the pressure on the body, and thus on the air in the lungs and on the oxygen and nitrogen dissolved in the bloodstream, is greatly increased. If, following a dive, the diver ascends to the surface slowly, the differing pressures inside and outside the body are gradually equalized without injury. If the diver breathes normally during such an ascent, the nitrogen dissolved in the bloodstream is also released gradually and is expelled by the normal action of the lungs.

If, however, a scuba diver ascends to the surface too rapidly, the air pressure in the lungs remains at a high level, while the external pressure on the body decreases rapidly. As a result, the air in the lungs expands rapidly and ruptures tiny vessels in the lungs. The air thus released can enter the space in the chest that contains the lungs, or the space in the chest that contains the heart, or it can enter the bloodstream and create a plug that blocks the normal flow of blood to the brain, heart, and other vital organs. An air bubble trapped in the bloodstream will often lodge in a joint, where blood vessels are smallest. Because of the differences in air pressure involved, air bubbles in the bloodstream can occur in dives as shallow as six feet.

A scuba diver suffering the effects of ascending too rapidly is likely to experience difficulty in breathing, pains in the chest, joints, or abdomen, dizziness, nausea or vomiting, and may also have a mottled coloration to the skin and exude a pink or bloody froth from the mouth and nose. The person normally will experience these difficulties immediately upon returning to the surface.

If a scuba diver fails to breathe normally during an ascent from a single or from repeated dives to a depth exceeding 60 feet for a total bottom time greater than 60 minutes, the nitrogen dissolved in the bloodstream is not expelled by the normal action of the lungs and can create bubbles in the bloodstream that block the normal flow of blood to the brain, heart, and other vital organs. A diver suffering from nitrogen bubbles in his or her bloodstream will exhibit the same signs as the diver suffering the effects of an air bubble, with two important differences: First, pain in the abdomen and joints will be so severe that the diver will actually double over, which gives this condition its name: "the bends." Second, a victim of the bends may not suffer difficulties until several hours after returning to the surface.

The emergency treatment for both types of scuba-diving injuries is the same:

If necessary, clear and maintain the victim's AIRWAY, restore BREATHING with MOUTH-TO-MOUTH VENT-ILATION, and restore CIRCULATION with CHEST COMPRESSIONS. Once the ABCs are restored, lay the victim on his or her left side to help keep the air or nitrogen bubbles in the bloodstream from migrating to the heart, elevate his or her feet eight to twelve inches to help keep the bubbles from migrating to the brain, keep the victim warm, and, if possible, administer pure oxygen. Call for help immediately and arrange to evacuate the victim to the nearest recompression chamber. If evacuation is to be by air, make certain the pilot understands that you suspect that the victim has air or gas bubbles in the bloodstream. The air pressure inside the aircraft should not exceed that experienced at 500 feet above sea level.

Burns

HEAT BURNS: If the victim's skin is red but not blistered or weeping, the injury is a first-degree burn, a burn that has injured only the top one or two layers of the skin. Immerse the affected area in cold (not ice) water or cover it with a cloth soaked in cold water for a short period. Apply an anaesthetic spray or ointment to relieve the pain. If necessary, apply a dry dressing, cover it with a bandage, and administer an oral pain medication such as aspirin or acetaminophen.

If the victim's skin is blistered or weeping, the injury is the deeper second-degree burn. Immerse the affected area in cold (not ice) water or cover it with a cloth soaked in cold water. Do not break any blisters that may be present; do not attempt to remove burned tissue; and do not apply any kind of antiseptic sprays or ointments. Apply only a dry dressing and a bandage. You may give the victim oral pain medication. If possible, keep the affected areas above the level of the victim's heart. If the affected area is extensive, it may be necessary to treat the victim for SHOCK.

If the victim's skin exhibits a white, gray, or black charring, he or she is suffering from the still deeper third-degree burn.

Do not attempt to remove any burned tissue or adherent clothing. If the affected area is extensive, do not immerse the victim in cold water or apply cold compresses, as cold could cause a significant fall in the body temperature. Shock may accompany third degree burns. If the affected area is limited, cold compresses may be applied. Do not apply any sprays or ointments. Apply only a dry, sterile dressing and a bandage and administer pain medication. If the affected area is the head or an extremity, elevate it above level of the victim's heart. If the burned area is large or deep, treat the victim for SHOCK (page115-117). Administer fluids as recommended for shock only if the victim is conscious and not vomiting and medical help is more than an hour away.

CHEMICAL BURNS: If necessary, remove the victim's clothing from the area of the burn and flush the affected area with water for at least five minutes. The eyes are extremely sensitive to chemical burns and should be treated in the same way Then, depending on the severity of the burn, treat the affected area as for a first-, second-, or third-degree heat burn, above.

Poisoning

POISONING BY MOUTH: If the victim is conscious, give him or her water or milk to dilute the poison. If medicinal charcoal is available, give that. Attempt to determine the source of the poisoning. If its container indicates a specific antidote, give it to the victim if it is available.

Do not attempt to administer fluids if the victim is unconscious.

If the source of the poisoning is unknown but is possibly an acid, alkali, or petroleum product, do not induce vomiting.

If a substance other than an acid, alkali, or petroleum product is known to be source of poisoning, induce vomiting by administering an emetic solution (for example, spirit of ipecac) or by poking your finger down the victim's throat. Then give milk or water to dilute what remains in the victim's stomach.

SEAFOOD POISONING: Shellfish such as shrimp, oysters, and clams can become infected with bacteria that can cause poisoning. The flesh of the puffer fish is poisonous. Victims of poisoning from shellfish or fish may experience a numbness around the face, especially around the mouth, weakness, increased salivation, increased thirst, and difficulty in speaking, which may indicate the onset of muscular paralysis.

Treat any suspected case of poisoning by mouth from seafood as poisoning with a noncorrosive substance: induce vomiting and dilute the poison with milk or other fluids.

Members of the tuna family (including mackerels) and large colored fish, such as strawberry grouper, contain ciguatera, which is also poisonous. Serious cases of ciguatera poisoning are marked by severe stomach cramps, often violent vomiting, excessive sweating, and a pale complexion. Some victims may become disoriented or hallucinate, and some may exhibit varying degrees of paralysis. A suspected victim of severe ciguatera poisoning must be transported to professional medical assistance as quickly as possible.

Many physicians are not familiar with treating ciguatera poisoning. If you encounter such a situation, you might inform the physician of the procedures suggested by Dr. Richard J. Lewis of Santa Monica, CA., an avid boater who has extensively researched ciguatera poisoning treatment. His recommendations, as published in the *Commodore's Bulletin* of the Seven Seas Cruising Association, are as follows: For severe cases, establish a 30 ml/hour flow of intraveneous saline or Ringer's solution, then piggyback 20 percent Mannitol at 500 ml/hour until symptoms disappear or to a maximum dosage of 5 ml/kg of the victim's body weight. The infusion of Mannitol should be interrupted if the blood pressure drops more than 15 mmHg. Symptoms usually respond to this treatment within ten minutes. For mild cases of ciguatera poisoning, Dr. Lewis recommends prescribing one 25 mg tablet of amitriptyline twice daily for two or three weeks.

POISONING BY INSECTS: For reactions to poisoning from insect bites or stings such as severe swelling, keep the affected area below the level of the victim's heart. Apply ice or cold cloths to the site of the bite and administer a mild pain-reliever such as aspirin or acetaminophen and for an antihistamine such as diphenhydramine (Benadryl™).

In the case of a sting by a wasp or hornet and bees other than the honeybee, scrub the area of the bite with soap and water, then attempt to remove the stinger and venom sac with a tweezers sterilized by immersion in alcohol or by heating over a flame and being allowed to cool.

The barbed stinger of a honeybee can continue to inject poison into the victim for up to twenty minutes after the initial attack. Do not use a tweezers to remove the stinger, as this squeezing action can inject more poison. Instead, remove the stinger by scraping it from the skin.

POISONING BY MARINE LIFE: TENTACLE STINGS by jellyfish, anemones, the Portuguese man-o'-war, and certain types of coral have stinging cells that can cause significant skin irritation, pain, nausea, vomiting, and muscle cramps.

First, flood the affected area with rubbing alcohol, ammonia, vinegar, or household bleach, which will help to inactivate the toxin. Second, if available, cover the affected area with meat tenderizer, which contains an enzyme that will destroy the toxin. Lastly, if available, cover the affected area with talcum powder or cornstarch, which will dry the skin and cause the stinging cells to stick together so you can scrape them from the skin.

PUNCTURE WOUNDS from such hazardous marine life as stingrays, sea urchins, cone shells, catfish, and stone, toad, weever, oyster, scorpion, zebra, and surgeon fish contain a toxin that is susceptible to heat. Immerse the affected area in water as hot as the victim can stand for 30 to 60 minutes. But be careful not to scald the victim, whose reaction to the toxin may temporarily negate any normal reaction to the pain of excess heat. (Test the water temperature with your own hand and make certain it is not too hot.)

Once the pain has subsided, flood the puncture wound with rubbing alcohol, ammonia, or household vinegar to deactivate the toxin. If medical help is more than six hours away, wrap the extremity above the wound in the direction of the heart with a mildly constrictive elastic bandage (not a tourniquet), to retard the flow of the toxin into the victim's vital organs. Appropriate treatments for poisoning by marine life are summarized in fig. 8.8.

POISONING BY PLANTS: Remove any of the victim's clothing that may have become contaminated by the plant's poisonous oils. Generously flush the affected area with water, then wash it with soap and water. If possible, follow this scrubbing with a flooding of rubbing alcohol, ammonia, vinegar, or household bleach diluted 50 percent with water. If a skin rash appears, apply calamine, aloe lotion, or cortisone ointment.

POISONING BY VENOMOUS SNAKE: Encourage the victim to sit or lie down and keep calm to slow the spread of the toxin

EMERGENCY TREATMENT OF INJURIES INFLICTED BY MARINE ANIMALS

Type of Injury	Marine Animal Involved	Emergency Treatment	Possible Complications
Major bite or laceration	Shark Barracuda Alligator gar	Control bleeding Cleanse wound Treat for shock Administer CPR Splint injury	Shock Infections
Minor bite or laceration	Moray Eel Turtle Corals	Cleanse wound Splint injury	Infections

Sting	Jellyfish
	Portuguese
	  man-o'-war
	Anemones
	Corals
	Hydra
		Inactivate the
		  toxin with
		  alcohol, meat
		  tenderizer
		Apply talcum
		  powder and
		  scrape
		  nematocysts
		  from skin
			Allergic
			  reactions
			Respiratory
			  arrest

Puncture	Urchins
	Cone shells
	Stingrays
	Spiny fish
		Soak in hot
		  water
			Allergic
			  reactions
			Respiratory
			  and circula-
			  tory collapse
			Infections
			Tetanus

Poisoning	Puffer fish
	Scrumboids
	  (tuna species)
	Ciguatera
	  (large, colored
	  fish)
	Shellfish
		Induce vomiting
		Give victim
		  water or milk
		Administer CPR
		Prevent self-
		  injury from
		  convulsions
			Allergic
			  reactions
			Asthmatic
			  reactions
			Numbness
			Temperature
			  reversal
			Respiratory and
			  circulatory
			  collapse

Figure 8.8

through the system. If the affected area is an arm or leg, wrap constricting bands (not a tourniquet) both above and below the bite to contain as much as possible of the toxin within the bite area. A pulse should still be detectable beyond the band farthest from the heart. Immobilize the arm or leg with a splint. Do not give the victim any fluids.

If possible, have your crew kill or capture the snake. Knowing what kind of snake caused the bite will be important to medical personnel in determining which antivenin to administer.

If the victim can be transported to medical care within 30 minutes, keep him or her lying down and calm and make the transport as quickly as possible. If possible, contact medical assistance and let them know you are on the way and what kind of snake was involved. In many locations, snake antivenin must be ordered from a central location (frequently a zoo or an aquarium), and your call will help speed the process.

If medical assistance is more than 30 minutes away, attempt to assess whether the snake actually injected a significant quantity of venom into the victim. If the bite area exhibits two distinct puncture wounds about an inch apart, it is probably from a pit viper, such as a rattlesnake, a copperhead, or a cottonmouth. If within five to ten minutes after the attack the victim does not experience a burning sensation at the site of the bite, it is unlikely that a significant quantity of venom was injected. Keep the victim calm and transport him or her to medical assistance as quickly as possible.

If the bite area exhibits two distinct punctures about an inch apart and the victim experiences a burning sensation at the site of the bite, a significant quantity of venom has probably been injected, which could be life-threatening. If medical assistance is more than 30 minutes away, you will have to suction as much of the venom out of the wound as possible. With a razor blade or sharp knife that has been sterilized in alcohol or by heating over a flame and being allowed to cool, make a one-half inch incision a quarter of an inch deep directly on top of each puncture wound. The cut should run along the long axis of the victim's affected body part to avoid cutting across muscle. If a snake-bite kit is available, use its suction cup to suction out the venom. If no snake-bite kit is available and you have no open cuts or sores in your mouth, suck and spit out as much of the venom as possible. Snake venom works through the bloodstream and is not harmful in the digestive tract. Transport the victim to medical assistance as rapidly as possible.

ANAPHYLAXIS: Many victims of certain types of ingested poisons or foods to which they are allergic, and of stings and bites from insects and hazardous marine-life, suffer a severe allergic reaction called ANAPHYLAXIS, which is type of SHOCK.

ANAPHYLAXIS is often marked by a flushing, itching, or burning of the victim's skin, especially in the face and upper chest; swollen welts spreading over the body; swelling of the face, tongue, and/or lips; and a bluish coloring to the lips. The victim may also experience a tightness or constriction in the chest; wheezing and/or coughing; and difficulty in exhaling.

Many individuals who are subject to such severe allergic reactions carry with them a small kit containing injectable epinephrine and an oral antihistamine. If such a kit is available, inject the epinephrine into a muscle in the victim's upper arm or hip. If the victim is conscious, administer the kit's oral antihistamine. Watch the victim closely. The injection of epinephrine may relieve the symptoms momentarily, but they may recur and the victim may require more injections of epinephrine or additional administrations of oral antihistamines.

If epinephrine and antihistamines are not available, the victim of ANAPHYLAXIS may well experience severe difficulties in BREATHING and may experience CARDIAC ARREST. If the victim stops breathing, open and maintain the AIRWAY (pages 105-106) and administer MOUTH-TO-MOUTH VENTILATION (pages 108-109). If there is no pulse, execute CHEST COMPRESSIONS (pages 109-111). Continue these steps until you are relieved by medical personnel or another rescuer, or you are exhausted.

Insulin Shock/Diabetic Coma

Glucose (sugar) is as vital as oxygen to the functioning of the brain. Brain cells deprived of glucose can suffer severe and permanent damage. Glucose enters the body in the foods we eat, but it cannot enter the body's cells without the presence of insulin, a hormone normally produced by the body itself.

Diabetics are individuals whose bodies produce no or insufficient levels of insulin. Diabetics whose bodies produce no natural insulin must inject insulin daily. Diabetics whose bodies produce insufficient levels of insulin often can control their condition by balancing their intake of glucose in the foods they eat or by taking pills.

Diabetics can suffer medical emergencies from either of two situations: INSULIN SHOCK, in which the level of glucose in their blood is too low; or DIABETIC COMA, in which the level of glucose in their blood is too high.

The signs of both conditions (fig. 8.9) are similar, which makes distinguishing between them and treating them appropriately very difficult. The primary difference, which will be readily apparent, is that the symptoms of INSULIN SHOCK often appear in a matter of minutes, while the symptoms of DIABETIC COMA normally appear over several hours. Diabetics are usually quite familiar with their disease and, if they are conscious, can tell you which condition they are suffering from and what you should do to help them.

INSULIN SHOCK: Of the two conditions, insulin shock is by far the more serious. If not treated promptly, severe brain damage can result. Insulin shock can be brought on if the victim takes too much insulin, takes a regular dose of insulin but does not eat enough food, or exercises excessively and uses up his body's available store of glucose. The victim of insulin shock usually will have pale, moist skin, will sweat profusely, will experience dizziness and/or headache, and may appear to be intoxicated, sometimes they will suffer a convulsion or seizure and/or lapse into unconsciousness.

The appropriate treatment for insulin shock is sugar. Fortunately, administering sugar to the victim of insulin shock is likely to correct his condition in a few minutes and prevent serious brain damage or death but does not create long-term harmful effects in the victim of diabetic coma.

For that reason, if you suspect either insulin shock or diabetic coma and the victim is conscious, give the victim sugar. The best way to administer sugar is in fruit juice, if possible sweetened with additional sugar; a candy bar, or even cake-decorating gel.

If the victim is not conscious, check and maintain his or her AIRWAY. If he or she suffers a convulsion or seizure, treat as detailed on pages 135-136 under CONVULSIONS and SEIZURES. Attempting to administer sugar in a liquid form such as fruit juice to an unconscious victim of insulin shock creates the danger of choking the person. However, if it will be more than 30 minutes before you can get the victim to professional medical assistance, you must get sugar in some form into his or her bloodstream. Place a glucose-laden substance such as refined sugar, syrup, or cake-decorating gel

SIGNS OF DIABETIC SHOCK OR COMA

Observation	Diabetic Shock	Diabetic Coma
Skin	Pale and moist	Warm and dry
Pulse	Normal, or rapid and full	Rapid and weak
Breathing	Normal or rapid	Gasping
Breath odor	Normal	Sweet or fruity
Thirst	Absent	Intense
Hunger	Intense	Absent
Vomiting	Unlikely	Likely
Headache	Present	Absent
Mood	Irritable	Restless
Food intake	Insufficient	Excessive
Insulin dosage	Excessive	Insufficient
Possible complications	Seizure or coma	Coma
Response to treatment	Immediate—after sugar administered	Gradual—within six to eight hours following medication

Figure 8.9

beneath the victim's tongue, allow it to dissolve, and replenish the supply often. Since the victim will not be able to swallow, place in the mouth only a small amount that will dissolve and be absorbed directly across the lining of the mouth; replace this frequently as needed or until the person returns to normal. Transport the person to medical assistance as quickly as possible.

DIABETIC COMA: The breathing of a victim of diabetic coma will often be rapid and consist of deep sighs; skin will be warm and dry; and breath may smell sweet or fruity. The victim may suffer a convulsion or seizure and/or lapse into unconsciousness. If any of those conditions are evident, open and maintain the victim's AIRWAY (pages 105-106), or treat as detailed below under CONVULSIONS AND SEIZURES.

Since the serious effects of diabetic coma develop over a period of several hours, transportation should be carried out as quickly as is practical but does not need to be conducted as an emergency evacuation. Remember, if you cannot distinguish between the two types of diabetic emergency, always treat the patient for insulin shock.

Convulsions and Seizures

Protect someone having a convulsion or seizure from injury but do not attempt to restrain the person. Loosen any clothing. If the victim's mouth is open, insert a soft object such as a rolled handkerchief between his or her back teeth. If the jaw is clenched, do not attempt to thrust an object between the teeth.

Most convulsions and seizures will last only a few moments, and your best course of action is simply to prevent the victim from getting injured and to observe him or her closely. Most victims will experience respiration difficulties during the attack. Maintain an open AIRWAY by using techniques described in the section on CPR (jaw thrust/chin lift). If the victim stops breathing, ventilate using a mouth-to-mouth or mouth-to-nose technique. (This is the same as MOUTH-TO-MOUTH VENTILATION, pages 108-109), but here you cover the victim's nose with your mouth.)

Once the convulsion or seizure has passed, the victim is likely to be exhausted and may be dazed or semiconscious. Allow the person to rest quietly and do not attempt to give any fluids until he or she is fully conscious.

If the victim has suffered convulsions or seizures in the past, the incident probably is not serious and requires no further intervention on your part. If he or she has forgotten to take anticonvulsant medication prescribed for seizures, give them as soon as the patient wakes up. If the victim has never suffered a convulsion or seizure before, the incident may well be more serious, transport the victim to medical assistance as quickly as possible.

Stroke

Stroke is the result of an insufficient supply of oxygenated blood to the brain. If the flow of oxygenated blood to the brain is interrupted for more than six minutes, irreversible damage is likely to occur in that portion of the brain that has lost its supply of oxygen.

Stroke can be caused by a gradual narrowing of the arteries that supply blood to the brain; by the blockage of these arteries by a blood clot that forms elsewhere in the body, such as in the heart; or by the rupture of an artery. The first two causes of stroke normally are associated with the elderly or with those who suffer from heart disease. The rupture of an artery serving the brain, however, can be the result of an inherent weakness in the artery and can occur suddenly and unexpectedly in young and otherwise healthy people.

The signs of stroke include partial or complete paralysis of the face muscles and/or the extremities on one side of the body (both sides of the body are rarely affected at the same time); varying levels of consciousness, ranging from confusion or dizziness to a total loss of consciousness; difficulties with speech, vision, or swallowing; convulsions; and headache.

Stroke victims often suffer paralysis of the airway following the incident. If you suspect stroke, immediately check and if necessary open and maintain the victim's AIRWAY (pages 105-106). A stroke victim is likely to be extremely frightened. Calm and reassure the victim as much as possible. If there is any paralysis, lay the victim with the paralyzed side down and pad all extremities carefully to avoid further injury.

There is nothing you can do aboard ship to relieve the symptoms of stroke or to determine its likely consequences, which can range from mild and temporary disability to severe disability and death. Any victim whom you suspect has suffered stroke should be evacuated to medical care as quickly as possible.

Eye Injuries

Small foreign bodies such as sand or grit lying in the lower half of the eye usually can be flushed away with clean water or a mild saline solution. Foreign bodies which have adhered to the eyeball or are lodged under the upper eyelid usually must be removed manually. Carefully try to remove the object from the eyeball with a cotton-tipped applicator or a small piece of gauze folded into a point. If it cannot be removed easily, flush with more water or saline and seek medical attention.

The victim of a blow to the eye from a blunt object may complain of difficulty in seeing or of double vision. The eye may bleed inside the covering of the eye. Have the victim lie down and close the injured eye, then cover that eye with a sterile dressing loosely taped in place. Since both eyes move together, also loosely tape a dressing over the uninjured eye to prevent unnecessary movement. Transport the victim to professional medical assistance as rapidly as is practical. The victim should remain lying down and stay as still as possible during transportation to avoid further potential injury.

If the eyeball has been penetrated by an object, make no attempt to remove it. Have the victim lie down. Do not apply any pressure to the eye, even if severe bleeding is present. If possible, place a paper cup or other protective covering over both the eye and the penetrating object and tape it in place. Loosely tape a dressing over the uninjured eye to prevent unnecessary movement. Have the victim lie as still as possible on his or her back and make the transport to medical assistance as quickly as is practical.

If the victim has suffered a chemical burn to the eyes, flush them with clean water continuously and thoroughly for ten to fifteen minutes. If only one eye is affected, turn the head so that the injured eye is lower than the uninjured eye, to avoid flushing the caustic solution into the uninjured eye. If pain or instinctive reaction prevents the victim from opening an injured eye wide enough to insure thorough and complete flushing, place your thumb as close as possible beneath the lower eyelid and your index finger at the top of his upper eyelid and force the eyelids to remain open during the flushing process. Once you have thoroughly flushed out the injured eye, cover both eyes with a loosely taped dressing and transport the victim to professional medical assistance as quickly as is practical.

Heatstroke and Heat Exhaustion

Persons exposed to high temperature, high humidity, and significant exertion may suffer from heat stroke and have abnormally high body temperature. They may act confused or disoriented or suffer complete loss of consciousness or even cardiac arrest. Move the victim to the coolest possible area; use fans or air conditioning if available. Remove all clothing and either immerse the victim in cold (not ice) water, cover him or her with towels soaked in cold water, or sponge off the skin with cold water until body temperature returns to normal. If the victim is conscious and not vomiting, administer liquids. Do not administer alcohol.

Hypothermia

Symptoms of hypothermia appear when the body's core temperature—normally 98.6° F—falls below 95° F.

As the body's core temperature drops, hypothermia progresses through five general stages:

1. When core temperature falls to between 90 and 95° F, the victim is likely to shiver, stamp his or her feet, and jump up and down in an effort to create additional internal heat. When the core temperature drops below about 90°F, shivering stops.
2. With a core temperature from 90 down to about 86° F, the victim exhibits a loss of small muscle activity, seen in syptoms such as a lack of coordinated finger motion.
3. As core temperature drops below about 85° F, the hypothermia victim becomes lethargic and sleepy and loses interest in battling the condition.
4. At a core temperature of around 80° F, the victim's pulse and respiration slow and become weaker. The victim may become irrational, then lapse into unconsciousness and finally into a coma.
5. When core temperature reaches 78° F, death can occur. However, recent incidents and studies have shown that when a core temperature is reduced rapidly (such as when individuals fall into icy water and become trapped), the body's metabolism can slow to remarkably low levels. Hypothermia victims have been revived after being deprived of oxygen for

several hours without apparent damage to their brain, heart, or other vital organs. For that reason, rescuers attempting to revive a hypothermia victim should continue resuscitation efforts until the victim's body temperature has risen to near normal levels and he or she still does not exhibit such vital signs as a heart beat, pulse, or breathing. Emergency medical technicians assume no hypothermia victim is dead until he or she is "warm dead."

Immediately remove a suspected victim of hypothermia from the cold environment.

If the victim is unconscious, check his or her respiration and pulse. If either is weak or absent, begin basic life support immediately by clearing an AIRWAY, pages 105-106, administering MOUTH-TO-MOUTH VENTILATION, pages 108-109,and, if necessary, CHEST COMPRESSIONS, pages 109-112.

As soon as respiration and a pulse are restored, move the victim to a warm area, strip away any wet clothing, and wrap the victim completely in warm blankets. Hypothermia victims whose core temperature has fallen low enough to weaken their respiration or pulse or trigger irrational behavior or unconsciousness can experience severe cardiac arrhythmia as their core body temperature returns to normal and must be transported as rapidly as possible to professional medical assistance. If medical help is more than 15 minutes away, attempt to arrange helicopter evacuation.

If a victim of mild hypothermia has not lost consciousness, has a strong respiration and pulse, and is alert and well-oriented, he or she is unlikely to require hospitalization. Make the victim rest, keep warm and dry, and drink small sips of warm liquids until external body temperature returns to normal.

Frostbite

Persons exposed to prolonged cold temperatures may actually freeze parts of their bodies (usually fingers and toes). These areas will be cold, hard, and numb. Transport the victim to shelter. If possible, warm the affected area by immersing it in tepid water, then gradually add warm water until the water temperature is between 102 and 105° F. If warm water is not available, warm the affected area by wrapping it in clothing or blankets. Do not rub the affected area, do not apply excessive heat, and do not allow the victim to expose the affected area to excess heat. Discontinue warming efforts as soon as normal skin color returns to the affected area. If normal color does not return to the affected area but the skin continues to exhibit a whitish color, transport the victim to medical assistance as quickly as possible.

Sea Sickness

While sea sickness itself is hardly a life-threatening emergency, extreme cases can lead to severe dehydration, which can have serious consequences.

The malady results from a disruption of the balance mechanism in the inner ear, which can be triggered by the motion of the vessel on the sea and/or by such visual signs as a tossing foredeck or rolling waves.

The best approach for individuals who are prone to sea sickness is to prevent its onset. Many individuals find the most effective preventative to be a patch affixed to the mastoid bone just behind the ear which slowly releases a dose of 0.5 mg. of scopolomine every 24 hours. These patches normally contain a total of 1.5 mg. of the drug and are designed to be effective for three 24-hour periods. Others find they are best helped by oral motion-sickness compounds such as Dramamine™ or Bonine™. Either of these preventatives should be employed at least four hours prior to embarking on any trip to sea, and either can cause extreme drowsiness and a dry mouth. Still other people have reported success from wristbands that purport to work by exerting force on an accupressure point, but their comfort may be more psychological than physical as there is little scientific evidence to support the claim.

Once at sea, anyone who begins to feel queasy should refrain from eating heavy foods or drinking alcoholic beverages. Some people do, however, find that nibbling on a soda cracker and sipping on a carbonated beverage helps to settle their stomach.

Individuals who feel a bout of sea sickness coming on should stay on deck rather than going below. Confinement in a closed space often makes the malady worse and can trigger vomiting, whereas fresh air often dissipates its symptoms. It's best if such individuals station themselves at the vessel's most stable point such as the cockpit of a sportfisherman rather than on its flying bridge. Focusing their eyes on the horizon rather than on the vessel or the sea tossing around them may also help restore a sense of equilibrium to the balance mechanism in their inner ear and cause the symptoms of sea sickness to subside.

Individuals who experience severe sea sickness to the point of actually vomiting often react in one of two ways: after the initial attack, some people "get their sea legs" and have no further problems; others find themselves completely unable to keep anything in their stomach and become caught up in a cycle of violent vomiting. If this goes on for more than 12 hours, it can lead to serious consequences from dehydration. The most dependable treatment is simply to return to shore. After a few hours on dry land, they normally will be able to take liquid nourishment and will recover without medical attention.

If returning to land is impossible (such as on a long ocean voyage) or does not relieve the symptoms, the most effective treatment is administration of Dramamine or Compazine™ suppositories. After the administration of two or three suppositories about four to six hours apart, the individual normally will be able to take enough liquids to avoid dehydration until they can reach land. Once onshore, they should seek professional medical help.

If You Need Medical Advice

If you encounter a medical emergency at sea that you do not feel qualified to handle without professional advice, you usually can make contact with a doctor through the Coast Guard on VHF Channel 16 or SSB frequency 2182 kHz. The Coast Guard has access to military and U.S. Public Health physicians and, through its AMVER system, keeps track of ships at sea that have medical staff aboard.

If you cannot reach the Coast Guard, try to contact Medical Advisory Systems, Inc. on SSB frequency 2182 kHz or one of the other SSB channels the company monitors, which are discussed on page 193.

When to Call for Emergency Evacuation

Evacuating a victim from your vessel to another vessel or a helicopter can be an extremely hazardous undertaking for the victim, for those aboard your own vessel, and possibly for the crew of the vessel or helicopter to which the victim is to be transferred, especially if the weather is rough.

Your decision whether or not to attempt emergency evacuation should be guided by the answers to five crucial questions:

- Does the victim require medical assistance that you cannot provide aboard your vessel in order to survive?

- How quickly must the victim get to that medical care in order to avoid serious medical consequences?

- How quickly can you transport the victim there aboard your own vessel?

- How quickly can the victim be transported there by another vessel or a helicopter?

- Is the difference between the time it will take you to get the victim to medical care and the time in which the victim can be transported to that care by another vessel or a helicopter sufficient to justify exposing the victim, your crew, and the crew of the rescue vessel or aircraft to the potential hazards of emergency evacuation?

Your answers to the first two of these questions depend on the nature of the victim's emergency and your estimation of the seriousness of his or her condition. Emergencies that place life in critical danger and about which you can do virtually nothing without advanced medical training and life-support equipment include: HEART ATTACK, STROKE, severe SHOCK, severe ANAPHYLAXIS, severe AIRWAY OBSTRUC-TIONS you cannot relieve, serious HEAD INJURY, severe INTERNAL BLEEDING, severe EXTERNAL BLEEDING you cannot control, significant OPEN CHEST or ABDOMINAL WOUNDS, significant THIRD-DEGREE BURNS, severe POISONING, and HYPOTHERMIA in which the victim has become irrational or lost consciousness. Transporting victims of these emergencies to medical care quickly and by any means that is safe and available is vital if they are to survive.

Your answers to the last three questions depend on circumstances: How far away from medical care are you? What is your vessel's maximum speed, and how long will it take you to transport the victim there? How soon can an emergency vessel or helicopter reach you? How severe is the weather and what hazards will it impose on the evacuation procedure?

If your answers to these questions convince you that emergency evacuation is necessary, state the nature of the emergency to potential rescuers clearly, be prepared to convince them, if necessary, that evacuation is truly necessary, and be certain that the position you give them for your vessel is accurate.

The actual procedures involved in helicopter evacuation are discussed fully on pages 65-73.

CHAPTER NINE

NAVIGATIONAL EMERGENCIES

- If relative bearing on another vessel remains constant, collision could be imminent. If yours is the burdened vessel, alter speed or course and, if required, sound appropriate audible signal.

- If navigational electronics fail, troubleshoot DC electrical system and try to restore function.

- If unable to restore electronics and unsure of position in daylight, stop vessel and try to determine position before proceeding.

- If unsure of position in darkness or fog, stop vessel, display appropriate lights and/or sound appropriate audible signals, and try to determine your position by visual or audible bearings on aids to navigation.

- **If relative bearings on another vessel remain constant, collision could be imminent. If yours is the burdened vessel, alter speed or course and, if necessary, sound appropriate audible signal.**

If a series of relative bearings on another vessel that is about to cross your course become progressively smaller (i.e., move towards your vessel's bow), the other vessel will cross ahead of you. If the bearings become progressively larger (i.e., move towards your vessel's stern), the vessel will cross astern of you. If the bearings remain constant (fig. 9.1), you are on a collision course. If yours is the privileged vessel, maintain speed and course; if yours is the burdened vessel, alter your course or speed to yield the right of way.

Determine whether yours is the privileged vessel, which

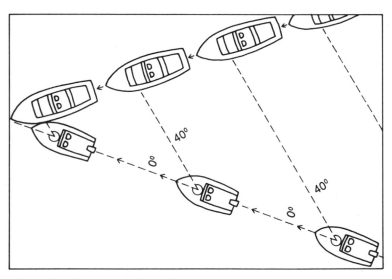

Figure 9.1 If a series of relative bearings on a vessel approaching you remain constant, you are on a collision course. If yours is the privileged vessel, maintain speed and course; if yours is the burdened vessel, alter your course or speed to yield the right of way.

has the right of way, or the burdened vessel, which must yield right of way, according to the following criteria:

In a crossing situation:

If you are proceeding under sail alone, your vessel is privileged over vessels operating under power. (Under the Rules of the Road, vessels "under power" include sailing vessels operating under an auxiliary engine, whether or not their sails are hoisted.) As a general rule, however, recreational vessels must yield the right of way to vessels engaged in fishing and to large commercial vessels that are restricted in their ability to maneuver.

If both yours and the other vessel are operating under either sail alone or under power, and you are to starboard of the other vessel, your vessel is privileged. If you are to port, you are burdened.

In meeting situations where yours and another vessel are approaching bow-to-bow within one point (11 1/4 degrees) of each other:

If you are under sail alone and the other vessel is under power, you are privileged. If you are under power and the other vessel is under sail alone, you are burdened. If both yours and the other vessel are operating under sail alone and you are on starboard tack, you are privileged. If you are on port tack, you are burdened.

If both you and the other vessel are operating under power, both of you are required to bear off to starboard with a single blast on your horn, which signals, "I intend to leave you on my port side."

- **If navigational electronics fail, troubleshoot DC electrical system and try to restore function.**

If all the DC electronic equipment aboard your vessel fails simultaneously, the problem is most likely in your battery, its controls, or its wiring system. If your vessel is equipped with a battery-paralleling switch, make certain it is turned to the battery serving your electronics. Check to see that the battery is full of acid. Make certain that the connections of its cables are clean and tight at the battery's terminals, where the battery's negative cable connects to ground, and the positive cable connects to your DC electrical panel. If the battery serving your electronics is completely discharged and you have another battery aboard, change the setting of the battery-paralleling switch to serve your electronics from a charged battery. If you have only one battery aboard and it is completely discharged, attempt to charge it off the engine alternator or an AC generator if you have one. Check the belt serving the engine alternator to make sure its tension is properly adjusted (see pages 156).

If several pieces of electronic equipment served off a common circuit in your DC electrical panel fail simultaneously, your problem is most likely in the connection between the battery and that circuit or in the DC electrical panel itself. Check to see that all connections between the battery and the circuit are clean and tight; check the fuse or circuit breaker serving that circuit, and check the connections at the circuit terminal itself.

If a single piece of electronic navigation equipment fails while other electronics served by that same circuit are functioning, the problem is most likely in the electronic equipment itself. Check to make certain that connections between the piece of electronic equipment and the DC electrical circuit serving it are tight and clean of corrosion.

Check the fuse of the electronic equipment itself, which may be in the back of the equipment's chassis or in its power line. Also check the connection where the equipment is grounded to make certain it is tight and free of corrosion. If the device is served by an antenna, check the connections between the equipment and the antenna and check the grounding of the antenna itself.

- **If unable to restore electronics and unsure of position in daylight, stop vessel and try to determine position before proceeding.**

If you can see land, try to determine your vessel's position by taking cross bearings on shoreside landmarks or aids to navigation.

If you are well offshore, try to determine your vessel's position by dead reckoning from your last known position. If your radio is working, request a fix of your position from any other vessel in sight or call the Coast Guard, which normally will be able to give you a bearing from their station, at least allowing you to establish a line of position.

If you are offshore, your radio is not working, no other vessels are in sight, and even your compass is not operating properly, try to determine the directions of the cardinal points of the compass from the angle of the sun and proceed towards the nearest land mass, then navigate to shore using dead reckoning.

- **If unsure of position in darkness or fog, stop vessel, display appropriate lights and/or sound appropriate audible signals, and try to determine position by visual or audible bearings on aids to navigation.**

First make certain that any other vessels in your vicinity are aware of your presence and position. If possible, display running lights. If your vessel's running lights are inoperative, post a lookout to signal with a portable light if you hear other vessels in your vicinity. In fog, if you are unable to show any lights, sound some audible signal at least once every two minutes, preferably with an air horn or bell. If you have neither aboard, bang two pots together.

If you are inshore, listen carefully for any audible signals from aids to navigation that might help you determine your position. If your radio is operative, call the Coast Guard, which should be able to give you a bearing from its station, at least allowing you to establish a line of position.

CHAPTER TEN

PROPULSION AND STEERING, LOSS OF

- If engine overheats or will not run, troubleshoot fuel, electrical, and/or lubrication/cooling systems to identify problem and attempt to remedy.

- If engine runs but vessel does not make headway when you shift to forward gear, shut down engine immediately and troubleshoot vessel's transmission, shafts, and propellers to identify the problem and attempt to remedy.

- If sailing vessel's standing or running rigging has been carried away, attempt to construct a jury rig.

- If vessel's steering has been damaged, try to repair it or construct a jury rig.

- Use dinghy for short-range emergency propulsion.

- If unable to restore sufficient propulsion to reach safety, use radio or audible or visual distress signals to summon assistance.

- **If engine overheats or will not run, troubleshoot fuel, electrical, and/or lubrication/cooling systems to identify problem and try to remedy.**

Reduced to its essentials, even the most elaborate gasoline (fig. 10.1) or diesel (fig. 10.2) marine engine is a fairly basic device that requires only three or four things in order to start and continue to operate: a source of motive power to get it started; a dependable source of clean, combustible fuel, and—in the case of a gasoline engine—electrical current to burn that fuel; and some means of dissipating the exhaust gases and excess heat generated by the engine. Both gasoline and diesel marine engines employ essentially the same

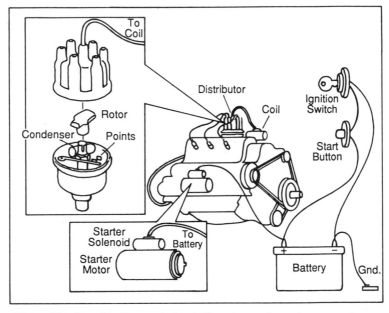

Figure 10.1 Use this diagram to locate the primary elements you must troubleshoot to identify a problem in the electrical starting or ignition systems of a gasoline engine.

starting system, which includes the engine's battery, the starter button and/or ignition switch, a starter solenoid, and a starter motor. (The starter solenoid and starter motor normally will be the two cylindrical units bolted to the side of the engine. The starter solenoid will be the smaller of the two and will be connected directly to the battery by the battery's positive—red—cable. In some cases, the starter solenoid is an integral part of the starter motor.) Both gasoline and diesel marine engines also use essentially the same type of lubrication and cooling system for dissipating the exhaust and excess heat the engines generate. Therefore, the troubleshooting procedure for identifying and solving some problems are the same for both gasoline and diesel marine engines.

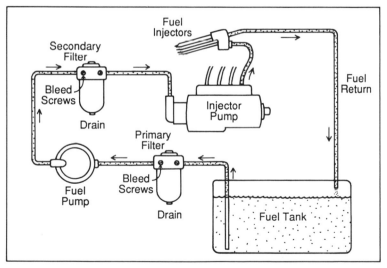

Figure 10.2 Use this diagram to locate the primary elements you must troubleshoot to identify a problem in the fuel system of a diesel engine.

Problem: You depress the engine start button or turn the ignition switch and nothing happens.

First check the battery. If your vessel is equipped with a battery-paralleling switch, make sure it is set to the battery serving the engine you are trying to start. Also make sure that the vessel's transmission is in neutral. (Most modern marine engines have a neutral safety switch that prevents the engine from being started if the transmission is in gear.) Make sure that the ignition switch is in the "on" position. If you have a voltmeter on board, check the voltage across the battery's positive and negative terminals. If you detect no, or almost no, voltage, the battery is dead and must be recharged from an external electrical source before it will develop sufficient voltage to start the engine.

If you do not have a voltmeter aboard, check the battery's acid level; if the battery's plates are exposed in one or more cells and the battery made no attempt to turn the engine's starter motor, it is probably fully discharged and is unlikely to generate enough voltage to start the engine without being recharged from an external electrical source.

On a vessel that has more than one battery, set the battery paralleling switch to "all" and try to start the engine with another of the ship's batteries. (If the engine starts, don't forget to reset the battery-paralleling switch to the engine's battery in order to recharge it.) If the vessel is fitted with an AC electrical generator, attempt to recharge the battery through the vessel's battery charger. If you have neither a charged battery nor an AC generator aboard and cannot start the engine by hand-cranking it, you have no chance of starting the engine. If you are inshore, you might try reaching safety by using your dinghy for auxiliary power (see page 170). If you are offshore, you will need to call for assistance.

On a 12-volt system, if your check of the battery's voltage with a voltmeter shows that it is charged to at least seven volts, and the level of battery acid is close to the fill ring, make certain that the cables connected to the battery's positive and negative terminals are tight and clean of corrosion. If not, clean and tighten them. Also make certain that the cable connected to the battery's negative terminal is clean and tight where it is connected to ground, and that the cable connected to the battery's positive terminal is tight and free of corrosion where it is connected to the starter solenoid.

Check the starter switch. If you found no problem with the battery, its controls, or its cables, check the starter button. First make sure that the wires connecting it to the battery and to the starter solenoid are clean and tight. If the starter button is connected to a separate ignition switch, also check the connections between them. If you have a voltmeter aboard, close the ignition switch (i.e., turn it to the "on" position) and check the voltage across its terminals. Or check it with the ignition switch in the "on" position by shorting across its terminals with a screwdriver. If you detect no voltage, or if the starter motor tries to turn, the switch itself is malfunctioning and you will have to bypass it to start the engine. If nothing happens, the switch is probably all right and the problem is either in the battery, the starter solenoid, or the electrical connections in the engine's starting circuit.

Check the starter solenoid. The starter solenoid serves two important functions: it delivers electrical current to the starter motor, and it mechanically engages the starter motor and the engine until the engine starts, then disengages them.

If you have a voltmeter aboard, close the ignition switch and check the voltage between the battery side of the starter solenoid and ground. On a 12-volt system, the starter solenoid should be receiving a minimum of seven volts of starting current from the battery. Check as well the voltage between the starter solenoid terminal serving the starter motor and ground, as well as the voltage between the starter motor terminal and ground. If you have lost voltage at any of those points, you will have isolated your problem, and you may be able to correct it by cleaning the appropriate terminal connections. If cleaning the terminals does no good, the electrical windings inside the starter solenoid are probably corroded and there is little you can do if you don't have a spare aboard. Call for assistance.

Problem: You turn the ignition switch or depress the engine start button and hear a clicking sound.

The problem is either low voltage in the battery or a mechanical problem inside the starter solenoid.

First check the condition of the battery. If you have less than seven volts across the battery's terminals, the battery will have to be recharged before it can start the engine, or you will have to use another of the vessel's batteries. If you have at least seven volts across the battery terminals, check all the connections among the battery, the ignition switch, and the starter solenoid. Corrosion at the connections could reduce voltage to the point that the starter solenoid will not turn the starter motor, which in turn will not crank the engine.

There are two other possible problems. One is that rust or corrosion has frozen the starter solenoid's helical spring or plunger, which engages the starter motor and the engine. Try rapping the starter solenoid sharply on its case two or three times with a heavy wrench to see if you can free the spring or the plunger. The other possible problem is that the starter motor is not firmly attached to the engine. It is that mechanical connection which provides the starter solenoid's ground. If the bolts securing the starter motor to the engine block are loose, clean off any corrosion and tighten them.

Problem: You turn the ignition switch or depress the engine start button and the starter motor struggles but will not crank the engine.

Check the voltage across the battery terminals and at all connections. On a 12-volt system, if you have at least seven volts at the starter motor terminal, either the starter motor is defective or one or more engine cylinders or its fuel line is locked with water, air, or gas vapor. If the blockage is in one or more engine cylinders, removing the spark plugs from a gasoline engine or the injectors from a diesel engine and trying to crank the engine will clear it. Clearing an air-lock on a diesel engine is covered below.

Problem: You turn the ignition switch or depress the engine start button and the engine starts but then stops as soon as you release pressure on the switch or button.

The ignition switch or start button is probably rigged with an auxiliary starting shunt whose ballast is defective. You will have to bypass the switch or button to start the engine and keep it running.

Problem: You can start the engine and it will run for a few minutes but quickly overheats.

Shut the engine down immediately and troubleshoot its lubrication/cooling system. Inspect the engine's dipstick to make sure that it has sufficient oil in the sump to keep it lubricated. If the oil in the engine sump is below the "full" mark on the dipstick, add oil, but be careful not to overfill the engine. Also check the oil on the dipstick for the presence of water. If water is detected, you may have a hole in the engine's water jacket. If that is the case, you probably also will notice an abnormally high reading on the engine's oil pressure gauge. There is nothing you can do to keep an engine with a ruptured water jacket from overheating, and you will have to call for assistance.

Check the engine's fresh-water cooling reservoir. This is just like checking the coolant in an automobile engine. Allow the engine to cool down before removing the reservoir's pressurized cap, as it could release steam and/or scalding water. If the reservoir is low, fill it to within about two inches of the neck. If the reservoir was low simply because you forgot to refill it before you left the dock, topping it off will probably solve the overheating problem. If the engine runs for a few minutes but overheats again, either the engine's fresh-water pump is malfunctioning or its raw-water cooling system is not operating properly.

To check the fresh-water pump, remove the plug on the side of its housing and make certain that it is full of water. If it is not, fill it and replace the plug. If the engine continues to overheat, the pump's impeller may be defective. If you have a spare impeller on board, install it. If you do not have a spare impeller on board, you will have to call for assistance.

To check the vessel's raw-water cooling system, look at the engine's exhaust outlet at the vessel's transom. When the engine is running, it should be discharging a significant stream of water. If it is, the raw-water cooling system is functioning properly. If it is not, the problem is probably a clogged or malfunctioning through-hull fitting or strainer on the raw-water inlet or a failed impeller in the engine's raw-water pump. To check the raw-water pump, loosen the clamps on the raw-water hose where it enters the engine's raw-water pump. If water begins to seep out of the junction, you probably have adequate raw water reaching the pump but its impeller has failed. If you have a spare impeller on board, install it. If you do not have a spare impeller, you will not be able to repair the pump and must call for assistance.

If water does not seep from the junction, carefully loosen the hose from the inlet of the raw-water pump. If no water gushes from the hose, the problem is most likely a clogged or malfunctioning raw-water strainer or inlet. Reattach the raw-water inlet hose to the raw-water pump and tighten its clamps. Close the sea cock or gate valve on the raw-water inlet and check the raw-water strainer. If it is clogged, clean it out. If the sea cock or gate valve serving the raw-water inlet is open, the raw-water strainer is clean, and the engine still overheats, the raw-water inlet is probably clogged and you will have to go beneath the vessel to remove the obstruction.

Problem: You turn the ignition switch or depress the engine start button and the engine turns over but will not fire.

If a vessel's engine doesn't start after turning over for about five seconds, don't just keep cranking it or you will run down the battery. Find out why it isn't starting and try to eliminate or solve the problem.

Since the engine turns over, the problem is not in its electrical starting circuit but in its ignition or fuel system. Here, the procedure you must follow for identifying and trying to solve the problem depends on whether you are dealing with an engine powered by gasoline or diesel fuel.

GASOLINE ENGINE

Begin by troubleshooting the ignition system: Remove a wire from one of the spark plugs. Hold it with some kind of insulating material with its end about a quarter of an inch from the engine block and try to start the engine.

If you do not see a spark when the engine turns over, the problem is electrical and is probably either a defective coil or a malfunction inside the distributor. The distributor will be a basically round housing that will have one wire leading into it and wires leading out of it to each spark plug. The wire leading into it will come from the coil.

To check the coil, remove the coil wire from the distributor cap, hold it in some kind of insulating material with its tip about a quarter of an inch from the engine block, and crank the engine.

If you see no spark, remove the distributor cap by releasing the spring clips at either side. This will reveal one or two sets of points and a small cylinder, which is the condenser. Tap the ignition switch or start button two or three times, which will cause the distributor shaft to rotate, which in turn should cause the points to open and close. If the points do not open and close, they may be fused together. Separate and clean them with a knife edge or sandpaper and tap the ignition switch or start button again to make sure they open and close properly. Tap the ignition switch or start button until the points make contact. Turn on the ignition switch or start button and separate the points with a screwdriver. Each time you separate them, a spark should jump between the end of the coil wire and the engine block.

If the points appear to be opening and closing properly but you do not see a spark at the end of the coil wire, either the coil or the condenser is defective. If you have a spare of the defective part aboard, install it. If you do not have a spare of the defective part aboard, you will not be able to start the engine and must call for assistance.

If you have a spark at the end of the coil wire but do not have a spark at the end of the spark plug wire, the problem lies in the distributor itself.

The inside of the distributor cap will be lined with one contact for each of the engine's cylinders. These contacts are energized in turn by a rotor, which receives current at its top from the coil wire and distributes it to each contact inside the distributor cap as it spins on the distributor shaft. Make certain the inside of the distributor cap is absolutely dry. If possible, spray it with a water inhibitor such as CRC™. Scrape down the contacts inside the distributor cap until they are shiny. Also scrape down the top of the rotor where it comes in contact with the coil wire, and its flat surface, which transmits the electrical current to each of the contacts inside the distributor cap. Reassemble the distributor cap, making certain that all the wires leading into it are seated securely and that the other end of the spark-plug wires are securely seated to the ends of the spark plugs.

If the engine still turns over but does not fire, the distributor cap is probably defective. If you have a spare distributor cap on board, install it. If you do not have a spare on board, you will not be able to start the engine and will have to call for assistance.

It's possible that the problem is in the spark plugs, but that is unlikely, since all the engine's spark plugs are not likely to go bad at once. If you have spark at the end of the spark-plug wire held about a quarter of an inch from the engine block, you can test the plugs by removing them from the block, reattaching their wires, laying them where you can see the gap at their business end, and cranking the engine.

If you have spark at the end of the spark-plug wire or at the end of the spark plug itself, either the spark is not hot enough to ignite the fuel, or the problem lies in the fuel system itself.

If the spark is not hot enough, the problem is either that the engine's generator or alternator is not putting out sufficient voltage or you have significant resistance somewhere in the ignition circuit, which is causing a voltage loss. Since you can't get the engine started, you can't check the output voltage of the generator or alternator. You can, however, check the belt driving the generator or alternator. Check its tension by pushing down on it halfway between the pulleys to which it is attached. If it is absolutely rigid, it could be freezing the alternator or generator rotor and will have to be loosened. If it deflects more than about an inch, tighten it. To adjust tension on the belt, loosen the bolts in the generator or alternator mounting bracket, pry the generator or alternator away from the engine block to tighten the belt or push it towards the block to loosen the belt, then resecure the mounting bolts.

Also recheck all terminals in the ignition system to be certain that you have eliminated all possible resistance.

After troubleshooting the ignition system, move on to the fuel system: If you have a spark at the spark plugs and the engine will turn over but not fire, the problem is probably in the vessel's fuel system.

Remove one of the engine's spark plugs. If its tip is wet, the engine's cylinders are flooded with gasoline. Wait about ten minutes to give the excess gasoline time to drain from the cylinders, then try to start the engine again.

If the engine still will not crank, you probably have an obstruction in the engine's fuel or air-intake system.

Remove the air filter, which normally sits on top of the carburetor, and try to start the engine. If the engine runs, a clogged air filter is your problem. If you have a spare filter aboard, install it. If you don't have a spare aboard, simply leave the air filter off the engine and replace it when you reach shore.

If replacing or removing the air filter does not solve your problem, visually check the carburetor fuel bowl. It should be full and the fuel clear.

If the bowl is empty, the carburetor is not getting fuel. Check to make certain you have fuel on board. If your vessel has a fuel manifold, make certain that you are feeding the engine from a tank which contains at least sufficient fuel to reach the level of the fuel pickup pipe. If you are sure you have sufficient fuel in the tank serving the engine, your problem may be a clogged fuel filter. Replace it with a fresh filter or remove it altogether. If you still do not see fuel in the carburetor bowl, check for a clogged fuel-line. Unscrew the fuel line between the fuel pump and the carburetor bowl and try to blow air through it. If you cannot easily blow air through it, clean the fuel line.

If you are certain you have fuel in the tank serving the engine but see no fuel in the carburetor bowl and cannot locate a plugged filter or fuel line, the problem is probably a defective fuel pump. If you have a spare fuel pump on board, install it. If you don't have a spare on board, you will have to call for assistance.

Diesel Engine

A diesel engine does not require an electrical ignition system to ignite its fuel; instead, it ignites its fuel by the heat of compression. A diesel engine, therefore, has no distributor, coil, points, condenser, or spark plugs. If a diesel engine will turn over but will not crank, the problem is most likely in its fuel system, which consists of a primary filter/separator, which removes large particles and water from the fuel; a fuel pump; a secondary filter, which removes small particles from the fuel; an injector pump; and the injectors themselves, which inject the fuel into the engine's cylinders. A diesel engine does not burn all the fuel that is fed to its injectors. For that reason, in addition to its fuel supply line, it also has a fuel return line through which unburned fuel is returned to the tank. The fuel supply line is susceptible to air-locks, which can prevent the engine from starting.

Begin your troubleshooting of the fuel system by first making sure that you have at least enough fuel in the tank serving the engine to reach the fuel pickup tube, and that any valves in the fuel system are in the open position. Make certain also that the throttle is in the start position. Many diesel marine engines are equipped with manual shutdown systems that stop the engine by shutting off its air supply. If the vessel has such a system, make sure its controls are set in the open position (i.e., that the plungers are pushed all the way into their seats). Some diesel marine engines are also equipped with mechanical or hydraulic governors. If the engine is equipped with such a device, make certain that the stop lever on the cover of a mechanical governor is in the "run" position; on a hydraulic governor, make certain the stop knob is pushed all the way in. If the engine is equipped with an air filter or breather, be sure it is not clogged.

Visually check the bowls housing the engine's primary and secondary fuel filters (some secondary filters are not housed in a bowl but are simply a screen-type filter in the fuel line itself); both should be full of fuel and the fuel should be clear. If you see excess water in the bowl of the primary filter, drain it off. If the primary filter bowl is full but the secondary filter bowl is empty, your problem may be a clogged primary filter; try replacing it. If both bowls are full, and the fuel in the primary filter bowl is clear but the fuel in the secondary filter bowl is dark, your problem may be a clogged secondary filter. Try replacing it.

If both filter bowls are empty, your problem is probably a malfunctioning fuel pump. If you have a spare fuel pump on board, install it. If you do not have a spare fuel pump on board, you will have to call for assistance.

If both filter bowls are full and the fuel is clear, your problem is probably an air-lock in the fuel-supply line. The housings for both the primary and the secondary filters should have bleed screws. Remove the bleed screw on the primary filter housing and attempt to start the engine. If air rather than fuel flows out the bleed-screw opening, let all the air escape before replacing the screw, then try to start the engine again. If that does not clear the lock, repeat the process with the bleed screw on the secondary filter housing. If you clear an air-lock but it reoccurs, make certain that all fittings along the fuel supply line are tight, check the seating of O-rings, and check the valves in both the primary and the secondary fuel filters.

If fuel flows from both bleed-screw openings when you remove the bleed screw but the engine still will not start, remove the fuel line from one of the injectors and try to start the engine. If fuel does not flow from the fuel line, your problem is probably a malfunctioning injector pump. If you have a spare injector pump aboard, install it. If you don't have a spare injector pump aboard, you will not be able to get the engine to run and will have to call for assistance.

- **If engine runs but vessel does not make headway when you shift to forward gear, shut down engine immediately and troubleshoot vessel's transmission, shafts, and propellers to identify problem and attempt to remedy.**

In the engine-room, check the coupling between the transmission and the propeller shaft. If it has come loose, tighten it. If it is broken and you have a spare coupling aboard, install it. If it is broken and you don't have a spare coupling aboard, you will have to call for assistance.

If the coupling is not the problem and you can go over the side, check the vessel's underwater gear. If the prop is fouled, clear it. With the engine off but the transmission in gear, attempt to rotate the propeller. If the propeller rotates while the shaft does not, you have sheared off the key that joins the two together. Replacing the key involves removing and replacing the propeller, which will be virtually impossible to do at sea. You will have to call for assistance. If both the shaft and the propeller rotate while the transmission is in gear, your problem is probably that the transmission itself is not engaging (see following paragraph). If neither the shaft nor the propeller turns, have a crew member shift the transmission to neutral and again try to rotate the propeller. If neither the propeller nor the shaft will turn, you probably have a frozen cutlass bearing. Replacing it at sea will be virtually impossible, and you will have to call for assistance.

If your troubleshooting up to this point indicates that your problem lies in the transmission, return to the engine-room and have a crew member start the engine and shift to forward gear while you check to see if the shaft exiting from the transmission is turning. If it is not, have a crew member shift the transmission from neutral to forward several times. If this does not engage the transmission, check the linkage between the helm control and the transmission itself. If it is mechanical, tighten it as necessary. If it is hydraulic, check the fluid level in the hydraulic pump and its fluid supply lines. Also check the level of fluid inside the transmission and top it off if it's low, but be sure not to overfill. If you find no problem with the transmission's linkage or fluid level, your problem is inside the transmission itself and there is little you can do to repair it. You will have to call for assistance.

- **If sailing vessel's standing or running rigging has been carried away, try to construct a jury rig.**

In any type of dismasting, salvage whatever you can of the downed rigging for your jury rig.

If your mast breaks above the spreaders and its lower shrouds are still in place, it's a fairly simple matter to jury-rig a sail on the portion that remains simply by creating new fore and after stays out of salvaged materials or out of dock or anchor lines. A broken gooseneck fitting can be temporarily replaced with lashings.

If your vessel's entire mast and boom have been carried away and cannot be salvaged, consider creating a new spar out of a whisker pole, dinghy oars lashed together end-to-end, or a boat hook.

In creating your jury rig, don't limit yourself to the traditional Marconi rig. A gaff or lateen rig may be easier to fashion out of the limited materials you have at hand. If land lies downwind, you might even be able to reach safety by rigging a simple square sail.

- **If vessel's steering has been damaged, try to repair it or construct a jury rig.**

If your vessel fails to answer its helm, first check to see if your rudder has been carried away or severely damaged.

If your rudder is still attached and will pivot, troubleshoot the steering mechanism.

On vessels with hydraulic steering, make certain the hydraulic fluid reservoir is full. If it is not, you probably have a leak in a hose, a fitting, or an O-ring somewhere in the system and will have to locate and repair it before you top off the reservoir. Even after you have stopped the leak and refilled the reservoir, you still may not have full steering control because of air trapped in the hydraulic lines. The hydraulic system should have an air-bleed valve in the fluid reservoir, the pump, or the lines. Locate it and bleed the air out of the system, then add enough fluid to the reservoir to replace the air you have expelled.

On vessels with mechanical steering, trace out the system to locate the problem, which most likely will be a broken cable, chain, clamp, or sprocket wheel. Once you identify the problem, replace the broken part if you have a spare on board, or try to rig a temporary repair that will hold together long enough to get you to shore. If yours is a sailing vessel with an inboard rudder, and you can't repair the steering mechanism itself, your best bet will be to lash a control line securely around the rudder blade and lead its bitter ends back to your cockpit winches.

If the problem is a broken tiller on a sailing vessel with an outboard rudder, lash up a temporary replacement out of whatever materials you have at hand, such as a dinghy oar. A pair of Vise-Grip™-type pliers is handy for getting a grip on a round rudder post.

The loss of rudders on a twin-screw power vessel can be temporarily offset by steering with the engines. But if the rudder of a single-engine vessel has been carried away entirely or its post has been so badly bent that it will not pivot, you probably will have to jury-rig a replacement. The easiest replacement to construct will be a sweep made from a hatch cover and a whisker pole or boat hook lashed to a vertical stanchion on the stern. A more difficult alternative is to rig a replacement out of lines and blocks.

• Use dinghy for short-range emergency propulsion.

If you are inshore and have a dinghy with an outboard motor, you may be able to use it to reach safety. Rather than trying to tow your vessel with the dinghy, lash it alongside (fig 10.3). If your vessel's steering system is working, the operation can be conducted in greater safety by lashing the dinghy's engine down in its fore-and-aft position and steering with your main vessel's controls. If your main vessel's steering is not operative, you will have to steer with the dinghy engine. If the weather is unsettled, wear a life jacket.

- **If unable to restore sufficient propulsion to reach safety, use radio or audible or visual distress signals to summon assistance.**

You normally will be able to summon assistance from the Coast Guard or a commercial towing service by calling them on VHF Channel 16 or SSB frequency 2182 kHz, then switching to a working channel. If you are unable to reach either the Coast Guard or a commercial towing service, broadcast a Pan-Pan urgency signal on VHF Channel 16 or SSB frequency 2182 kHz. If other boaters who might be able to render assistance are nearby, employ visual and audible distress signals to attract their attention.

Tips on Towing and Being Towed

Unless towing operations are conducted carefully and with proper procedures, they can be dangerous to both of the vessels involved and to their crews. Here's the right way to do it:

- If possible, use braided nylon for the towing line. For a given diameter, it is stronger than three-strand-twist nylon line and has more elasticity to absorb the shocks and strains of towing. When three-strand-twist nylon breaks under a heavy load, it snaps back like a whip and can inflict serious injury on crew members aboard either vessel.

- Using a bridle aboard the towing vessel will distribute the strain and help the vessel being towed to track in a straighter line. The bridle should not, however, be rigged to the towing vessel's stern, as it will severely restrict the towing vessel's maneuverability.

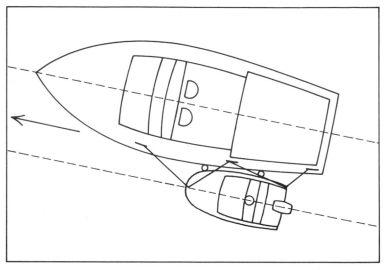

Figure 103 Lashing a dinghy alongside a disabled main vessel as "get-home" power makes it more manageable than using it as a towing vessel.

Instead, rig the ends of the bridle as far forward on the towing vessel as possible in order to leave the stern free to turn as needed. Wrap the line where it comes into contact with the towing vessel's house to keep it from marring the surface. Rig the bitter end of the towing line to both forward cleats on the vessel being towed and lead it as nearly as possible directly over the vessel's bow rather than off to either side.

• Post lookouts on both vessels to watch the tow line, but be certain that they are positioned well clear of the line to avoid injury in case it breaks and whips back. The lookout on the towing vessel should be especially alert to keep the line from fouling the towing vessel's propeller.

- The vessel to be towed will track straighter if it is trimmed slightly by the stern (i.e., if weight is shifted aft) to keep its bow light. The vessel being towed should keep an anchor ready for instant deployment in case the tow line breaks.

- The towing vessel should take up slack on the tow line slowly and begin the tow with just enough power to overcome the two vessels' inertia. Once under way, it should maintain a moderate speed to keep the vessel being towed from yawing.

- If any sea is running, adjust the length of the tow line to keep both vessels synchronized on the crests or in the troughs of successive waves. If the two vessels are not properly spaced, the towing vessel will run down the face of one wave while the vessel being towed is struggling up the back of the next wave, creating maximum resistance. Conversely, while the towing vessel is struggling up the back of one wave, the vessel being towed will run down the face of the wave behind, possibly resulting in a collision.

- If the towing vessel is to bring the vessel being towed to a dock, come to a gradual stop a good distance off. The impaired vessel should then be pulled up to the towing vessel with the tow line. Never try to fend off either vessel with hands or feet, which could become trapped between the two hulls and broken or crushed. Lash the two vessels together so they will both respond to the towing vessel's steering. This will allow the towing vessel to bring the vessel being towed to the dock under control rather than out of control at the end of a long tow line.

- If the towing operations must be conducted at night, the towing vessel should shine a searchlight on the vessel being towed to warn other vessels in the vicinity of the relationship between the two vessels.

- If the towing operation must be conducted in fog, the towing vessel should sound one prolonged blast and two short blasts on her horn every two minutes. If the vessel being towed is manned, it should sound one prolonged blast and three short blasts on its horn immediately following the towing vessel's signal.

CHAPTER ELEVEN

RADIOS, EMERGENCY USE OF

- If vessel or life of anyone on board is in grave and imminent danger, transmit Mayday distress call and message immediately.

- If within 20 miles of shore, transmit Mayday distress call and message first on VHF Channel 16 (156.8 MHz).

- If more than 20 miles from shore and vessel is equipped with single-sideband marine radiotelephone, transmit Mayday distress call and message first on SSB frequency 2182 kHz.

- If possible, precede every transmission of Mayday distress call and message with international radiotelephone alarm signal.

- If you have transmitted Mayday, then find you no longer require assistance, see that it is canceled.

- Transmit Pan-Pan urgency call and message only to communicate that safety of a vessel or person is in jeopardy, but the danger is not life-threatening.

CONTINUED

- Transmit Securite safety signal over a distress frequency only to alert others to information concerning safety of navigation or important meteorological warnings. Transmit Securite safety message on a working channel.

- In absence of other assistance, for advice on handling a serious medical emergency on board, contact Medical Advisory Systems, Inc. (MAS) on SSB frequency 2182 kHz.

For emergency steps to follow upon receiving a Mayday Distress Call and Message see pages 194-201.

- **If vessel or life of anyone on board is in grave and imminent danger, transmit Mayday distress call and message immediately.**

The importance of getting off a Mayday distress call and message the instant a serious emergency strikes aboard your vessel is best illustrated by the experience of my friend Sumner Pingree when a turbo-charger fire erupted aboard his 53-foot sportfisherman, *Roulette*, off the coast of Puerto Rico (see pages 34-36). "By the time my son was halfway up the flying bridge ladder to tell me about the fire, smoke was everywhere," he told me later. "I immediately got off a Mayday call to the Coast Guard. I said I was not declaring an emergency but asked them to stand by. We opened the engine-room door, and the fire reignited with a whoosh. I raced back up to the flying bridge to call the Coast Guard again, but the fire had already burned through the battery cables and the radio was dead. Ten minutes after we first realized we had a fire aboard, we were swimming. I was amazed by how quickly she burned." Had Sumner waited to transmit a Mayday distress call and message until he assessed the damage the fire had caused, he would have found that his radio had already been knocked out of commission.

The Mayday distress call and message has absolute priority over all other radio traffic.

Once you decide to transmit a Mayday, do so using the complete format (fig. 11.1). Do not omit any items or use any other format. The first distress call and message you transmit may be the only one you are able to transmit, and this format quickly, clearly, and concisely provides the essential information that potential rescuers will need.

Any time you are involved in distress radio traffic, whether on your own behalf or in rendering assistance to others, the last thing you want to do is compound the

FORMAT FOR TRANSMITTING
Mayday DISTRESS CALL AND MESSAGE

Fill this form out for your vessel. Speak SLOWLY—CLEARLY—CALMLY.

1. Activate international radiotelephone alarm signal.

2. "MAYDAY—MAYDAY—MAYDAY."

3. "THIS IS _____, _____
              (your boat name)   (your boat name)

   _____, _____."
              (your boat name)   (your call sign)

4. "MAYDAY: _____."
              (your boat name)

5. "POSITION IS: _____."
              (your vessel's position in degrees and
              minutes of latitude NORTH or SOUTH and
              longitude EAST or WEST; or as distance and
              bearing [magnetic or true] to well-known
              navigation landmark)

6. "WE _____."
              (state nature of your emergency)

7. "WE REQUIRE _____."
              (state type of assistance required)

8. "ABOARD ARE _____."
              (give number of adults and children on
              board and conditions of any injured)

9. "_____ IS A _____-FOOT
     (your boat name)   (length of your boat in feet)

   _____ WITH A _____
     (type: sloop, motor yacht, etc.)   (hull color)

   HULL AND _____ TRIM."
              (color of trim)

10. "I WILL BE LISTENING ON CHANNEL 16/2182."
               (cross out channel or frequency that does not apply)

11. "THIS IS _____, _____."
               (your boat name)   (and call sign)

12. "OVER."

Figure 11.1

situation with inaccurate, incomplete, or incomprehensible transmissions. The quality of distress transmissions may well be poor. Remain calm and take extra care to speak slowly, clearly, and distinctly. Use radio transmission procedure words properly and be careful to pronounce them correctly. (You'll find a list of procedure words, their meanings, and correct pronunciation in fig. 11.10, on pages 207-208.) If you feel there is any doubt that you will be understood, use phonetic spelling. (The phonetic spelling alphabet is in fig. 11.11, on page 209.)

Technically, the Mayday distress call and message procedure consists of three elements:

1. The international radiotelephone alarm signal.
2. The distress call, consisting of:
    (a) The distress signal MAYDAY, spoken three times;
    (b) The words: This Is...;
    (c) The name of the vessel in distress, spoken three times;
    (d) The radio call sign of the vessel in distress spoken once.
3. The distress message, consisting of:
    (a) The distress signal MAYDAY, spoken once;
    (b) The name of the vessel in distress, spoken once;
    (c) The position of the vessel in distress, expressed as degrees and minutes of latitude North or South and longitude East or West, or by bearing (specify whether true or magnetic) and distance to a well-known reference point, such as an aid to navigation or shoreside landmark;
    (d) The nature of distress;
    (e) The type of assistance required;
    (f) Any other information that might facilitate rescue, such as:

- The number of adults and children on board
- The injuries suffered by anyone on board and the medical assistance they require.
- The length of the vessel
- The type of vessel (sloop, motor yacht, etc.)
- The color of the vessel's hull, superstructure and trim

4. The word "over" indicates the conclusion of the call and requests a response.

If your Mayday is acknowledged and you are uncertain of the extent of your emergency, ask the vessel or station you have contacted to stand by. If, as in Sumner's case, the emergency escalates rapidly and knocks out your radio, you will at least know that someone is aware that you are in trouble and knows your position, the nature of your distress, and the number of persons on board, and has a description of your vessel. Even if you lose the ability to receive before hearing an acknowledgment, you have the hope that someone heard your message but was unable to acknowledge it in time.

The Mayday distress call and message should never be transmitted in any but the most extreme emergencies—those that pose genuine and serious dangers to your vessel or that threaten the lives of your crew. Situations such as being lost, having someone aboard suffer a serious but not life-threatening illness or injury, mechanical difficulties, or running out of fuel are not sufficient justification for transmitting a Mayday unless any of those factors places your vessel or crew in immediate and serious danger.

Anyone foolish enough to transmit a Mayday for frivolous or nonexistent reasons is subject to significant criminal and civil penalties. Using your radiotelephone to transmit a false Mayday subjects you to a fine of up to $10 thousand and/or up to a year in jail and can result in the loss of your FCC radiotelephone operator license for life. In addition, the Coast Guard has prosecuted individuals who transmitted false Mayday distress calls and messages and has succeeded in obtaining judgments against them to recover costs of resulting search-and-rescue efforts that ran into the thousands of dollars.

Do not transmit the Mayday distress call and message in a man overboard situation, even if you require the assistance of other vessels. Instead, transmit the Pan-Pan urgency call and message (see page 189 for a brief summary and pages 189-190 for details).

- **If within 20 miles of shore, transmit Mayday distress call and message first on VHF Channel 16 (156.8 MHz).**

VHF radio waves travel only in a line-of-sight, and 20 miles is about the maximum distance over which you can reliably expect to communicate with an installed VHF marine radiotelephone. (Its range may be considerably greater if you are within line-of-sight of a tall receiving antenna on shore. If your VHF antenna is ten to fifteen feet off the water, for instance, and is in line-of-sight of a 2,000-foot-high receiving antenna on shore, your radio's range under optimum conditions could be as much as 75 miles, but you don't want to bet your life on it.)

If you encounter a serious emergency well offshore and do not have a marina single-sideband radio aboard, you should of course transmit your Mayday distress call and message on your VHF radiotelephone, as there is always the possibility that your transmission will be received by another vessel within a 20-mile radius of your position. But again, you don't want to trust your vessel or your life to that kind of gamble.

If you are within 20 miles of shore and in an emergency serious enough to require you to transmit the Mayday distress call and message, you may use any VHF channel to attract attention. Your first choice, however, should be Channel 16, which is the International Distress, Safety, and Calling channel both ship-to-coast and intership and is continuously monitored by the Coast Guard.

After transmitting the distress call and message on VHF Channel 16, wait 30 seconds for any vessel receiving it to respond. If no answer is received, retransmit the distress call and message over that same channel.) If no answer is received following that transmission, try Channel 6 (156.3 MHz, the intership safety channel). If you still receive no acknowledgment, retransmit the distress call and message on any VHF channel frequently used in the area. One method is to scan the VHF channels until you hear traffic, then break into the traffic with your Mayday distress call and message. If you do not hear traffic on any VHF channel, try transmitting your Mayday on Channel 22A (157.1 MHz), the primary Coast Guard liaison channel, or Channel 72 (156.625 MHz), which at sea is used as an international ship-to-ship channel. If you still receive no acknowledgment and have time, try one or more of the Public Correspondence channels. The Public Correspondence channels used vary from area to area, but the primary ones are Channel 26 (ship's transmit frequency, 157.3 MHz; ship's receive frequency, 161.9 MHz) and Channel 28 (ship's transmit frequency, 157.4 MHz; ship's receive frequency, 162.0 MHz).

• **If more than 20 miles from shore and vessel is equipped with single-sideband marine radiotelephone, transmit Mayday distress call and message first on SSB frequency 2182 kHz.**

Any vessel that ventures more than 20 miles offshore should be equipped with a good SSB marine radio. In an emergency serious enough to require you to transmit the Mayday distress call and message, you may use any SSB channel or frequency to attract attention. Your first choice, however, should be frequency 2182 kHz, which is the SSB International Distress, Safety, and Calling frequency both ship-to-coast and intership and is continuously monitored by the Coast Guard.

After transmitting the distress call and message on 2182 kHz, wait 30 seconds for any vessel receiving it to respond. If no answer is received, retransmit the distress call and message over that same frequency. If no answer is received following that transmission, retransmit the distress call and message on any SSB frequency used in the area. Good second choices would be 2670 kHz, a primary Coast Guard working channel, and ITU Channel 424 (ship's transmit carrier 4134.3 kHz; ship's receive carrier, 4428.7 kHz) or ITU Channel 816 (ship's transmit carrier, 8241.5 kHz; ship's receive carrier, 8765.4 kHz), both of which are continuously monitored by the Coast Guard as part of its Contact and Long Range Liaison (CALL) system.† If no acknowledgment is received, scan the

---

† On July 1, 1991 at 0000 hours UTC, the transmit and receive frequencies for virtually all ITU channels in the 4 megahertz band and above will change by about 100 kHz. After that moment, the frequency pairs of factory-programmed ITU channels in marine SSB radios will no longer be correct and cannot be used. (Neither the 2182 kHz International Safety, Distress, and Calling frequency nor 2670 kHz, the Coast Guard's primary SSB working channel, will be effected.) The frequencies of factory-programmed SSB channels may be altered only by a technician with an appropriate FCC license. In the month prior to the date of the changeover, you should have at least some of the frequency pairs in each of the megahertz bands covered by your SSB radio reprogrammed to the new frequencies for use after the changeover. You should have the frequency pairs in the remaining factory-programmed channels reprogrammed to the new frequencies in the month following the recommended changeover.

HIGH SEAS COAST STATION FREQUENCIES†

KMI (Point Reyes, California)

ITU Channel	Ship Transmit Carrier	Ship Receive Carrier
242 *	2003.0	2450.0
248 *	2406.0	2506.0
401	4063.0	4357.4
416	4109.5	4403.9
417	4112.6	4407.0
804	8204.3	8728.2
809	8219.8	8743.7
822	8260.1	8784.0
1201	12330.0	13100.8
1202	12333.1	13103.9
1203	12336.2	13107.0
1229	12416.8	13187.6
1602	16463.1	17236.0
1603	16466.2	17239.1
1624	16531.3	17304.2
2214	22040.3	22636.3
2223	22068.2	22664.2
2228	22083.7	22679.7
2236	22108.5	22704.5

WLO (Mobile, Alabama)

ITU Channel	Ship Transmit Carrier	Ship Receive Carrier
405	4075.4	4369.8
414	4103.3	4397.7
419	4118.8	4413.2
824	8266.3	8790.2
829	8281.8	8805.7
830	8284.9	8808.8
1212	12364.1	13134.9
1226	12407.5	13178.3
1641	16584.0	17356.9
2237	22111.6	22707.6

CONTINUED

Figure 11.2

WOM (Fort Lauderdale, Florida)

ITU Channel	Ship Transmit Carrier	Ship Receive Carrier
209 *	2031.5	2490.0
221 *	2118.0	2514.0
245 *	2390.0	2566.0
247 *	2406.0	2442.0
403	4069.2	4363.6
412	4097.1	4391.5
417	4112.6	4407.0
423	4131.2	4425.6
802	8198.1	8722.0
805	8207.4	8731.3
810	8222.9	8746.8
814	8235.3	8759.2
825	8269.4	8793.3
831	8288.0	8811.9
1206	12345.5	13116.3
1208	12351.7	13122.5
1209	12354.8	13125.6
1215	12373.4	13144.2
1223	12398.2	13169.0
1230	12419.9	13190.7
1601	16460.0	17232.9
1609	16484.8	17257.7
1610	16487.9	17260.8
1611	16491.0	17263.9
1616	16506.5	17279.4
2215	22043.4	22639.4
2216	22046.5	22642.5
2222	22065.1	22661.1

CONTINUED

(Figure 11.2)

† See note on page 183.

* In the 2 and 3 megahertz SSB bands, channel designations and transmit and receive frequency pairs are not controlled by international treaty but by individual nations. Channel designations and frequency pairs may vary from country to country and even from region to region within a single nation's jurisdiction.

WOO (Manahawkin, New Jersey)

ITU Channel	Ship Transmit Carrier	Ship Receive Carrier
232	2166.0	2558.0
242	2366.0	2450.0
410	4090.9	4385.3
411	4094.0	4388.4
416	4190.5	4403.9
422	4128.1	4422.5
808	8216.7	8740.6
811	8226.0	8749.9
815	8238.4	8762.3
826	8272.5	8796.4
1203	12336.2	13107.0
1210	12357.9	13128.7
1211	12361.0	13131.8
1228	12413.7	13184.5
1605	16472.4	17245.3
1620	16518.9	17291.8
1626	16537.5	17310.4
1631	16553.0	17325.9
2201	22000.0	22596.0
2205	22012.4	22608.4
2210	22027.9	22623.9
2236	22108.5	22704.5

(Figure 11.2)

ITU channels used by the High Seas Stations and break in to any traffic you hear with your Mayday. If you hear no traffic, you can try transmitting your Mayday over one or more of the channels used by the High Seas Stations, but to have a reasonable chance of being heard you will have to select an appropriate megahertz band, based on your distance from the station and on the time of day. A list of all the channels used by the High Seas Stations will be found in fig. 11.2.

- If possible, precede every transmission of Mayday distress call and message with international radio-telephone alarm signal.

The radiotelephone alarm signal consists of two audio frequency tones transmitted alternately for a duration of one-quarter of a second each. One tone must have a frequency of 2200 Hertz and the other a frequency of 1300 Hertz. Transmitted together, they sound something like an ambulance siren. Many modern VHF and SSB marine radios are equipped with an automatic international radiotelephone alarm that is activated by pressing a clearly marked button on the front of the radio's panel. A radiotelephone alarm signal generated automatically must be transmitted for at least thirty seconds, but not more than one minute. Its purpose is to alert the attention of a person on watch and to activate certain automatic equipment.

With one exception, the radiotelephone alarm must be transmitted from a vessel only to announce that a Mayday distress call and message will follow. The single exception to that rule is that it may be used to precede a Pan-Pan urgency call and message involving a man overboard where assistance is required that cannot be satisfactorily obtained by the use of the urgency call and message without preceding it with the radiotelephone alarm signal.

- If you have transmitted Mayday, then find you no longer require assistance, see that it is canceled.

If after transmitting a Mayday you find that you are able to handle the emergency without assistance, and you have not delegated control of the distress traffic to another vessel or coast station, you must cancel your distress call and message whether or not it was acknowledged. If your Mayday was acknowledged by the Coast Guard or other appropriate

FORMAT FOR CANCELLING A **Mayday** DISTRESS CALL AND MESSAGE BY A VESSEL

To cancel a Mayday distress call and message that you, as a vessel in distress, previously transmitted when the cancellation cannot be accomplished through a coast station:

1. "MAYDAY"
2. HELLO ALL STATIONS, HELLO ALL STATIONS, HELLO ALL STATIONS."
3. "THIS IS_____, _____."
           (your boat name)   (your call sign)
4. "THE TIME IS:_____."
           (state time of transmission by 24-hour clock)
5. "_____, _____."
           (your boat name)   (your call sign)
6. "SEELONCE FEENEE."
7. "_____, _____."
           (your boat name)   (your call sign)
8. "OUT."

To cancel a Mayday distress call and message you have previously transmitted on behalf of a vessel in distress, although you were not in distress yourself.

1. "MAYDAY"
2. "HELLO ALL STATIONS, HELLO ALL STATIONS, HELLO ALL STATIONS."
3. "THIS IS_____, _____."
           (your boat name)   (your call sign)
4. "THE TIME IS:_____."
           (state time of transmission by 24-hour clock)
5. "_____, _____."
      (the name of the vessel and call sign of the vessel in distress)
6. "SEELONCE FEENEE."
7. "_____, _____."
           (your boat name)   (your call sign)
8. "OUT."

Figure 11.3

FORMAT FOR TRANSMITTING
Pan-Pan
URGENCY CALL AND MESSAGE

1. "PAN-PAN PAN-PAN PAN-PAN" (properly pronounced PAHN-PAHN).

2. "ALL STATIONS" (or the name of a particular vessel).

3. "THIS IS_____, _____."
                (your boat name)   (your call sign)

4. "WE _____."
       (state nature of your emergency)

5. "WE REQUIRE _____."
            (state type of assistance required or give other useful information such as your position, a description of your vessel, or the number of people on board)

6. "THIS IS_____, _____."
                (your boat name)   (your call sign)

7. "OVER."

Figure 11.4

authority, contact them in the normal, nonemergency way and inform them of the cancellation. They will then usually transmit a "notification of resumption of normal working." If your Mayday was not acknowledged by the Coast Guard or other appropriate authority, or you cannot contact the authority that acknowledged your Mayday, you are required to cancel it using the format described in fig. 11.3.

- Transmit Pan-Pan urgency signal and message only to communicate that safety of a vessel or person is in jeopardy, but the danger is not life-threatening.

The Pan-Pan urgency signal and the message that follows it have priority over all other transmissions except the Mayday distress call and message. The urgency signal may be transmitted to a specific vessel or "to all stations." The proper format for transmitting the Pan-Pan urgency signal and message will be found in fig. 11.4.

A typical situation in which you would transmit the Pan-Pan urgency signal "to all stations" would be one in which a person falls overboard from your own vessel and you require the assistance of other vessels to retrieve him. That is the only emergency in which the Pan-Pan urgency call and message may be preceded by the radiotelephone alarm, and even then the alarm should be used only if you feel you cannot satisfactorily obtain the assistance you require through the urgency signal alone.

A typical situation in which you would address the Pan-Pan urgency signal to a specific vessel would be one in which you see a person fall overboard from that vessel and no one aboard that vessel appears to be aware of the accident.

Another example of the proper use of the urgency call and message would be a situation in which your vessel has struck a submerged object and is taking on water but is not in imminent danger of sinking. If you feel the situation might become serious enough to require assistance, transmit the Pan-Pan urgency call and message to alert rescue services or other vessels in your vicinity that you may need their help. Still another example would be a situation in which your vessel has lost power or steering in a busy traffic area and could pose a hazard to other vessels.

If you transmit the Pan-Pan urgency signal addressed "to

FORMAT FOR CANCELLING A
Pan-Pan
URGENCY CALL AND MESSAGE
BY A VESSEL

1. "PAN-PAN PAN-PAN PAN-PAN."

2. "HELLO ALL STATIONS, HELLO ALL STATIONS, HELLO ALL STATIONS."

3. "THIS IS_____, _____."
                    (your boat name)   (your call sign)

4. "THE TIME IS:_____."
                  (state time of transmission by 24-hour clock)

5. "_____, _____."
          (your boat name)   (your call sign)

6. "SEELONCE FEENEE."

7. "_____, _____."
          (your boat name)   (your call sign)

8. "OUT."

Figure 11.5

all stations," you must cancel it by transmitting the cancellation on that same frequency using the format in fig. 11.5. If you addressed the urgency signal to a specific vessel, its cancellation is not required.

- **Transmit Securite safety signal over a distress frequency only to alert others to information concerning safety of navigation or important meteorological warnings. Transmit Securite safety message on a working channel.**

The Securite safety signal and message are mostly transmitted by coast stations to warn of hazards to navigation or severe weather systems. However, they may also be transmitted by vessels. The safety signal is transmitted on a distress channel with instructions for receiving stations to switch to a working channel. The safety message is then transmitted over the working channel specified in the safety signal.

A typical example of a situation in which you might transmit a safety signal and message would be one in which you spot a large submerged object that could pose a serious danger to other vessels. You should first try to contact the

---

FORMAT FOR TRANSMITTING
Securite
SAFETY CALL AND MESSAGE

To transmit the SECURITE safety signal:

Transmit on VHF Channel 16 or SSB frequency 2182 kHz:

1. "Say-curiTAY—Say-curiTAY—Say-curiTAY—ALL STATIONS."
2. "THIS IS _____, _____."
                    (your boat name)   (your call sign)
3. "LISTEN:_____."
               (state working VHF channel or SSB frequency)
4. "_____OUT."
               (your call sign)

To transmit the SECURITE safety signal:

Transmit on working VHF channel or SSB frequency designated above:

1. "Say-curiTAY—Say-curiTAY—Say-curiTAY—ALL STATIONS."
2. "THIS IS _____, _____."
                    (your boat name)   (your call sign)
3. "_____."
               (state securite message)
4. "_____OUT."
               (your call sign)

Figure 11.6

Coast Guard to alert them to the danger, and they will then probably transmit a Securite signal and message concerning it on VHF Channel 22A. If you are unable to reach the Coast Guard and feel that the object poses sufficient danger to require notifying other vessels in the area, find a working channel such as VHF Channel 6, 68, or 72 that is not in use. Then transmit a Securite signal over a distress channel (inshore you normally would transmit on VHF Channel 16; offshore, on SSB 2182 kHz) and instruct receiving stations to switch to the working channel you have selected. Switch to the working channel you specified in the Securite signal and transmit the safety message, which should include a description of the object, its location, its approximate depth below the surface, and the direction in which it is drifting, if any. An example of the proper format for transmitting the Securite safety signal and message is given in fig. 11.6.

• In absence of other assistance, for advice on handling a serious medical emergency on board, contact Medical Advisory Systems, Inc. (MAS), on SSB frequency 2182 kHz.

In most cases, you will be able to obtain advice on handling medical emergencies on board through a call to the Coast Guard. If for any reason you can't contact them and have a serious medical emergency, such as a heart attack, you can call Medical Advisory Systems, Inc. (MAS). This private company operates the Medical Telecommunications Response Center in Owings, Maryland, which is staffed around the clock by its own physicians. It serves primarily commercial marine vessels and remote industrial locations that subscribe to its services, but it will provide assistance to nonsubscribers in a genuine and serious emergency. (Don't call them if a member of your crew gets a splinter.)

IF YOU RECEIVE A MAYDAY DISTRESS CALL AND MESSAGE

- If your assistance is required to prevent loss of life at sea, you are legally obligated to provide it as long as you can do so without serious danger to your own vessel or crew.

- If you receive the Mayday distress call and message from vessel undoubtedly in your vicinity, you must immediately acknowledge it.

- If you acknowledge receipt of the Mayday distress call and message, you must respond to it.

- Under certain circumstances, if you learn that a vessel is in distress, you must relay the Mayday distress call and message, even if not in a position to assist.

If you are within range of a VHF marine operator, you can call MAS at (301) 257-9504. Offshore, you can contact them at that number on your SSB marine radio through a High Seas marine operator. The company also continuously monitors SSB frequencies 2182 kHz and 16590.0 kHz, and scans five others: 4983.0 kHz, 7952.0 kHz, 12327.0 kHz, 16450.0 kHz, and 22722.0 kHz.

- If your assistance is required to prevent loss of life at sea, you are legally obligated to provide it as long as you can do so without serious danger to your own vessel or crew.

Under federal law,† as the person in charge of a vessel in waters subject to U.S. jurisdiction or of an American flag-vessel operating on the high seas, you are legally required to render assistance to any individual found at sea "in danger of being lost" as long as you can do so without serious danger to your own vessel or crew. If you fail to render such assistance, you are liable to a fine of up to $1 thousand, or two years imprisonment, or both.

- **If you receive the Mayday distress call and message from a vessel that beyond any possible doubt is in your vicinity, you must immediately acknowledge it.**

This is a rule of the Federal Communications Commission. The lone exception to it is that, if you are in an area where reliable communication between the vessel in distress and a coast station is "practicable," you may defer your acknowledgment for a "short interval" so that a coast station may acknowledge receipt.

The conventional wisdom on this topic says that if you receive a Mayday, you should do nothing, just listen. I strongly disagree. If I were in an area where there was the least doubt about the ability of a vessel in distress to reach a coast station and I received a Mayday call from a vessel anywhere near me, I would acknowledge it as quickly as the distress message was concluded and I could get to my radio's microphone. My reasoning is twofold: first, the FCC says that under that set of conditions I "must immediately" acknowledge; second, if I were the hapless soul in deep enough trouble to be transmitting the Mayday, I would want

---

† Public Law 98-89, Duty to Provide Assistance at Sea, enacted by Congress August 26, 1983 (46 U.S. Code 2301-2304)

FORMAT FOR ACKNOWLEDGING
Mayday DISTRESS CALL AND MESSAGE

On channel or frequency over which you received the MAYDAY:

1. "_____, _____, _____."
   (name of vessel in distress, spoken three times)

2. "THIS IS_____, _____, _____, _____."
   (your boat name, spoken three times) (your call sign)

3. "RECEIVED MAYDAY."

4. "OVER."

Figure 11.7

anyone who received my call to respond as quickly as possible. If I were that person and had time to transmit my distress message only once, it would be reassuring to know that someone had heard me and was sending the cavalry in my direction.

The FCC rules do not define just what constitutes the "short interval" you are required to wait if you receive a Mayday in an area where reliable communication between a vessel in distress and a coast station is practicable. I would acknowledge receipt of any Mayday distress call and message if it were not acknowledged by someone else within about 15 seconds.

If you are called on to acknowledge a Mayday distress call and message, do so using the format found in fig. 11.7.

If you acknowledge receipt of a Mayday distress call and message and a legitimate authority such as the Coast Guard later comes on the channel, you should state your vessel's name and call sign and ask them if they wish you to continue to attempt to provide assistance to the vessel in distress or simply stand by on that frequency in case your assistance is required.

If you receive a Mayday distress call and message from a vessel that is undoubtedly not in your vicinity, the FCC rules say you must allow a "short interval" of time to elapse before acknowledging receipt of the call and message to allow stations nearer the vessel in distress to acknowledge them without interference. Again, the FCC does not define "short interval," but if I heard a Mayday from a vessel I knew was far away from me, and no one else acknowledged it within about 15 seconds, I would.

The FCC rules state that anyone who hears a Mayday must immediately cease any transmission capable of interfering with the distress traffic and continue to listen on the frequency over which it was transmitted. The rules do not, however, say how long you are required to listen. If the vessel in distress were in my vicinity, if its distress call had been acknowledged by a coast station, and if I apparently were the vessel best positioned to render possible assistance, I would alter my course in the direction of the vessel in distress and attempt to contact the controlling coast station through normal, nonemergency means. If I were able to contact the coast station, I would inform the personnel there of my position, ask if I could help, and follow their instructions. If I were unable to contact the controlling authority by nonemergency means, I would get back on the frequency carrying the distress traffic, wait for a break, quickly inform the controlling authority of my position and ask if my assistance were required, then follow their instructions.

If another vessel apparently in a better position to assist were involved in the distress, my actions would be determined by the situation. If I felt there was any reasonable chance that my assistance might be required, I'd steam towards the vessel in distress and inform the controlling authority of my availability to assist if needed. If there appeared to be little likelihood that my assistance would be required, I'd continue on my course but monitor the frequency until I heard the message announcing resumption of normal working. If I clearly were not in a position to assist, I'd probably continue to monitor the distress traffic as a matter of personal interest, making certain that I did nothing to interfere with it, but otherwise would go about my normal business.

Though the FCC regulations no longer require non-commercial vessels to keep a radio log, you are required to log any Mayday calls you receive. Enter the date, time, your location and the message received in your regular ship's log.

The FCC rules do state that if you hear a Pan-Pan urgency signal you must continue to listen on the frequency over which it was broadcast for three minutes. If no message follows the urgency signal, or if the message following it is not addressed to "all stations," after three minutes you may resume normal working. Beyond that, the FCC rules get a little murky. They say that if the urgency message was addressed to "all stations," the vessel that transmitted it must cancel it as soon as it knows action is no longer required. The rules are silent, however, on what those who have heard the urgency signal are supposed to do. If the emergency were in my vicinity, I'd monitor the channel over which the urgency message was transmitted until I heard the cancellation or was pretty certain that no action on my part was required. If the emergency were clearly well away from me, I'd probably go back to normal working.

- **If you acknowledge receipt of the Mayday distress call and message, you must respond to it.**

Once you have acknowledged receipt of a Mayday distress call and message, you not only are required by federal law to respond, but are also required by FCC rules to transmit an

---

FORMAT FOR OFFER OF ASSISTANCE MESSAGE
IN RESPONSE TO A
Mayday DISTRESS CALL AND MESSAGE

On channel or frequency over which you acknowledged receipt of the MAYDAY distress call and message:

1. " _____ ."
    (the name of the vessel in distress, spoken once)
2. "THIS IS _____ ."
          (your boat name)
3. "OVER."

On hearing the word "OVER" from the vessel in distress, continue:

4. "I AM _____ ."
    (state your intentions: i.e., "PROCEEDING TOWARD
    YOU FROM TEN MILES. EXPECT TO ARRIVE IN ONE
    HOUR")
5. " _____ ."
    (state other useful information: i.e., " COAST GUARD
    HAS BEEN NOTIFIED, INCLUDING YOUR NEED FOR
    DOCTOR")
6. " _____, _____ ."
    (your boat name)   (your call sign))
7. "OVER."

Figure 11.8

offer-of-assistance message to the vessel in distress as soon as possible. (Wait long enough to allow coast stations or other vessels to respond to the Mayday and to work out your own position relative to the vessel in distress and formulate your intentions.)

The proper format for your offer of assistance message is found in fig. 11.8.

If, after you transmit your offer of assistance and are under way to provide assistance, a legitimate authority such as the Coast Guard enters the search and/or rescue effort, state your vessel's name and call sign and ask the authority whether they wish you to proceed or simply stand by ready to render assistance if it should be required.

- **Under certain circumstances, if you learn that a vessel is in distress, you must relay the Mayday distress call and message, even if you are not in a position to assist.**

According to the FCC rules, you must relay a Mayday distress call and message in the following circumstances:

1. When the vessel in distress cannot transmit the distress call and message herself.

2. When you believe that further assistance is required.

3. When you hear a distress message that has not been acknowledged, even if you are not in a position to assist. In this case, you must also try to notify an appropriate authority, such as the Coast Guard, of the distress message you have received.

The proper format for relaying a Mayday distress call and message is given in fig. 11.9. Note that it should be preceded, if possible, by the radiotelephone alarm.

Control of Distress Radio Traffic

If you transmit a Mayday and it is acknowledged by the Coast Guard or another appropriate authority, that authority normally will assume control of any radio traffic related to the distress. If your Mayday is not acknowledged by the Coast Guard or another appropriate authority, you are the controller of the distress traffic. You may retain that control

---

**FORMAT FOR RELAYING
Mayday DISTRESS CALL AND MESSAGE**

1. Activate radiotelephone alarm signal.
2. "MAYDAY RELAY—MAYDAY RELAY—MAYDAY RELAY."
3. "THIS IS_____, _____, _____, _____."
      (your boat name, spoken three times) (your call sign)
4. "_____."
      (state the distress message: I.e., the name of the vessel
      in distress, its position, the nature of the distress, the
      nature of assistance required, and any other useful
      information such as a description of the vessel, the
      number of people on board, and any injuries they have
      sustained.)
5. "I WILL BE LISTENING ON CHANNEL 16/2182."
      (cross out the channel or frequency which does not
      apply).
6. "_____, _____."
      (your boat name)   (your call sign))
7. "OVER."

Figure 11.9

yourself or you may delegate it to another vessel.

Controlling distress traffic involves certain responsibilities. The station controlling the distress traffic has the authority to impose silence on the frequency being used for distress traffic on all vessels or coast stations that might interfere with the distress traffic. Such imposition of silence may be addressed to "all stations" or to an individual vessel or coast station, followed by the words "Seelonce Mayday". No further instructions or identification of the controlling station are required, and the Seelonce Mayday order must be respected.

If essential, any other vessel in the vicinity of the vessel in distress—even though it has not been delegated as the station controlling the distress traffic—may also impose radio silence on the frequency with the words "Seelonce Distress" followed by that vessel's own call sign and/or vessel name.

Troubleshooting Guide to Marine Radios

In an emergency, a VHF or SSB marine radio does not do you any good if you can't transmit and receive over it. If you need your radio for emergency communications and it doesn't seem to be working properly, here are some things to quickly check:

1. Is your ship's service battery system working properly?

   A) If none of the equipment that is powered by your ship's service battery is working, the problem is probably with the battery itself. Check to see that it is filled with water and that the cables connected to it are tightly affixed and not corroded. If necessary, refill the battery with water and/or remove, clean, and reattach the battery cables securely.

   B) If some, but not all of the equipment powered by your ship's service battery is working, the problem is probably in your vessel's electrical distribution panel. Trace your radio's power cable to its connection at the distribution panel. Check the fuse or circuit breaker serving the terminal to which the radio's power cable is connected. If your distribution panel uses fuses, check the fuse in the circuit serving your radio. It normally will be a small, clear-glass tube with metal caps on either end, each of which snaps into a small pair of prongs. A thin wire or small strip of metal will run through the glass tube lengthwise. If either of the metal caps at the ends of the fuse shows signs of a chalky green or white substance, it is corroded.

Remove the fuse from the prongs into which it snaps and scrape both the cap and the prongs down to bright, shiny metal. (Be careful not to allow any metal such as a knife blade or screwdriver to contact the sets of prongs that hold the two ends of the fuse at the same time. You could get an electrical shock.) Hold the fuse up to a light and shake it gently. If the wire or metal strip is broken or loose, replace the fuse with another of the same type and size.

If your distribution panel uses circuit breakers, check to make certain that the breaker is not tripped and, if necessary, reset it.

If after any of these steps you still doubt that the terminal is delivering power to your radio, disconnect the radio's power cable and attach it to a circuit serving working equipment that is powered by your ship's service battery, such as a loran receiver or a knotmeter.

If your radio seems to be the only piece of equipment powered by your ship's service battery that isn't working, the problem is probably with the radio's electrical power supply, its antenna system, or the radio itself.

1. Is the radio turned on?

    Make sure the radio's "power" switch is in the "on" position. If the power switch is on and the radio is working, the lights on its front panel should be glowing. The fact that the lights are glowing indicates that the radio is getting some electrical power, but the fact that they aren't glowing doesn't necessarily mean the radio isn't transmitting or receiving properly. If the lights aren't glowing but you can receive any noise over the radio, even just static, the light bulbs or the circuit board to which they are connected could be burned out, loose, or disconnected, or their contacts could be corroded. If the lights aren't glowing and you can't receive even static over the radio, turn the power switch on and then off several times. It may be shorted out or corroded. If so, you will have to remove the radio from its case to clean, tighten, or replace the switch.

2. Is the radio connected to an adequate source of power?

    If the radio's front panel lights aren't glowing and you can't receive even static over it, check its fuse. The fuse can either be in the back of the radio case behind a small knob marked "fuse" or housed in a cylindrical fitting in the radio's power cable. If so, the fitting usually will be about an inch long and half an inch in diameter and will be black. Once you have located the fuse, unscrew the knob or the fitting, remove the fuse, and check it and its contacts as suggested above for a fuse in the distribution panel. If one or both of the metal caps on the ends of the fuse are corroded, clean them and their contacts inside the fuse housing. If the wire or metal strip inside the fuse is loose or broken, replace the fuse.

3. Is the radio properly connected to a functioning antenna?

    A) A marine radio will not transmit or receive adequately if it is not properly connected to a functioning antenna. Check the lead from your radio to the base of its antenna to make sure the connections at both ends are securely tightened and are not corroded. If necessary remove, clean, and re-secure them. Check along the length of the antenna lead to make sure it is not broken.

B) Check the antenna itself to make certain that it has not been damaged or swept away. In either case, connect the radio's antenna lead to an emergency replacement antenna or construct a jury rig. In the case of a VHF radio, a random length of wire will function as a jury-rig antenna. Preferably it should be about six feet long. It must be oriented vertically and installed as high on your vessel as possible.

You can also jury-rig an antenna for your marine single-sideband radio, provided you have an automatic antenna tuner installed between the jury rig and the radio. A sailboat's backstay or forestay can be used, but before connecting the lead from the antenna tuner to it, make sure the radio is turned off, as the jury rig will carry a significant amount of electrical current. Once you have made the connection, warn your crew to stand well clear of the jury rig, or they could receive a nasty electrical shock.

4. Is the radio transmitting?

A) If the radio appears to be receiving adequate power from your ship's service battery and to be properly connected to an undamaged or jury- rigged antenna, you may find you can receive over it but cannot transmit. When you depress the microphone's transmit button, a light on the radio's front panel marked "transmit" should glow. The fact that the "transmit" light glows indicates that you are transmitting, but the fact that it does not doesn't necessarily mean you aren't transmitting. The bulb may simply be loose, its base corroded, or it could be burned out. Push on the bulb and wiggle it to see if you can establish contact. If not, you will have to either disassemble the radio to clean the bulb's contacts or replace the bulb. The best indication that you are not transmitting is that although you are able to receive on a channel, when you transmit on it you receive no acknowledgment.

B) Activate the microphone's transmit button several times to see if the "transmit" light comes on. The button itself may be loose or corroded. If so, you will have to disassemble the microphone to clean, tighten, or replace it.

C) Check any external connection between the microphone and the radio itself. Some microphones are attached to their radios by a connector that can become loose or corroded. If your microphone has such a connector, make certain it is not corroded and is securely tightened. If necessary, clean and retighten it.

If none of the above steps convinces you that your radio is working properly, about your only recourse is to remove the radio from its case and check inside for any signs of corrosion on any of its terminals, or for loose or disconnected wires. Before removing the radio from its case, make certain you disconnect its power supply to avoid the possibility of electrical shock.

RADIO PROCEDURE WORDS

AFFIRMATIVE   You are correct, or what you have transmitted is correct.

BREAK   I separate the text from other portions of the message; or I separate one message from another which follows immediately.

FIGURES   Figures or numbers follow. Used when numbers occur in a message, such as: "*Ladye Anne* is figures four eight, repeat figures four eight feet, in length".

I SPELL   I shall spell the next word phonetically. (see figure 11.11: Phonetic Spelling Alphabet)

MAYDAY   The international distress signal indicating that a vessel or a person is in grave and imminent danger. Spoken three times. (MAYDAY is the accepted English pronunciation of the French word m´aidez, "help me.") The MAYDAY distress call and message have priority over all other transmissions.

NEGATIVE   You are not correct, or what you have transmitted is not correct.

OUT   This is the end of my transmission to you, and no reply is required or expected.

OVER   This is the end of the currrent portion of my transmission to you, and your response is necessary and expected.

PAN-PAN   The international urgency signal indicating a vessel or person is in jeopardy but the danger is not life-threatening. The phrase is spoken three times. Properly pronounced: "PAHN-PAHN," the PAN-PAN urgency signal has priority over all transmissions except the MAYDAY distress signal.

CONTINUED

Figure 11.10

ROGER	I have received your last transmission satisfactorily and understand your message.
SECURITE	When used as the international safety signal, it is spoken three times and properly pronounced SaycuriTAY. The SECURITE safety signal has priority over all other transmissions except the MAYDAY distress signal and the PAN-PAN urgency signal.
THIS IS	This transmission is from the station whose name and/or call sign immediately follows.
SILENCE	When used to order the cessation of interfering transmissions over a channel or frequency being used for emergency communications, SILENCE is correctly pronounced "SEE-LONCE" and is spoken three times.
SILENCE FINI	Used to signal the resumption of normal working on a channel or frequency previously used for distress communications. Pronounced SEE-LONCE FEE-NEE.
WAIT	I must pause for a few minutes. Stand by for further transmission.

(Figure 11.10)

PHONETIC SPELLING ALPHABET

LETTER	WORD	SPOKEN AS	LETTER	WORD	SPOKEN AS
A	Alfa	AL fah	N	November	No VEM ber
B	Bravo	BRAH vo	O	Oscar	OSS ker
C	Charlie	CHAR lee	P	Papa	PAH pah
D	Delta	DEL tah	Q	Quebec	Keh BECK
E	Echo	ECK oh	R	Romeo	ROW me oh
F	Foxtrot	FOKS trot	S	Sierra	See AIR rah
G	Golf	GOLF	T	Tango	TAN go
H	Hotel	Hoh TELL	U	Uniform	YOU nee form
I	India	IN dee ah	V	Victor	VIK ter
J	Juliet	JEW lee ETT	W	Whiskey	WISS kee
K	Kilo	KEE low	X	X-ray	ECKS ray
L	Lima	LEE mah	Y	Yankee	YANK ee
M	Mike	MIKE	Z	Zulu	ZOO loo

(Figure 11.11)

APPENDICES

Recommended Medical Supplies

Item	*Quantity*
Alcohol	2 bottles, 16 oz. ea.
Ammonia inhalents	12
Analgesic ointment	4 tubes, 2oz. ea.
Analgesics	600 tablets/capsules
Antacid	2 bottles, 16 oz. ea.
Antibiotic ointment	4 tubes, 1 oz. ea.
Antidiarrhea compound	2 bottles, 16 oz. ea.
Antiemetic compound	2 bottles, 16 oz. ea.
Bandages, adhesive	2 large boxes of assorted sizes
Bandages, elastic	4, 4" x 4' ea.
Bandage scissors	1 pair
Bee-sting kit	1
Benadryl	50 tablets, 25 mg. ea.
Benzocaine toothache gel	4 tubes, 1/3 oz. ea.
Betadine scrub brushes	24
Betadine solution	2 bottles, 4 oz. ea.
Bronchodilators	2
Cake decorating gel	4 tubes, 16 oz. ea.
Charcoal, liquid activated	2 bottles, 16 oz. ea.
Chemical heat packs	24
Chemical ice packs	24
Chlorine bleach	2 bottles, 6 oz. ea.
Ear drops, nonprescription	2 bottles, 1 oz. ea.
Ear syringe	1
Eye drops, nonprescription	4 bottles, 1 oz. ea.
Gauze pads	1 box of 100, 4" x 4" ea.
Ipecac	2 bottles, 16 oz. ea.
Lip balm, medicated with sunscreen	10 tubes, 1.5 oz. ea.
Meat tenderizer	2 bottles, 4 oz. ea.
Mineral oil	1 bottle, 16 oz.
Needle-nose tweezers	1 pair

Nosebleed packs	6
Oral thermometers	2
Penlight	1 (with extra batteries)
Safety pins	24 in assorted sizes
Scopolamine patches	1 box of 50
Snakebite kit	1
Sunscreen lotion containing PABA	4 bottles in assorted strengths
Sunburn lotion	6 bottles, 8 oz. ea.
Throat lozenges	100
Tape, waterproof	1", 100 feet ft.
	2", 100 feet ft.
Vinyl gloves	1 box of 50 ea.

TRAUMA KIT

The following recommendations are intended as a general guide to the equipment that would be required aboard a vessel intended for offshore cruising to allow an appropriately trained crew member to provide basic trauma life support for at least 24 hours until the victim can be transported to professional medical assistance. Specific items should be employed only after appropriate training in their use has been completed and, if at all possible, only under the direction of a qualified physician. Purchases of the recommended equipment should be made through a competent surgical supply house that can ensure that necessary equipment and systems are compatible and complete. The recommendations cover only adults. If small children will be aboard, sizes and dosages must be altered appropriately.

General Supplies:

Item	Quantity
Alcohol wipes	1 box of 200
Bandages, elastic	4, 4" x 6' ea.
Bandages, elastic, self-adhering pressure	4
Bandages, roller	12
Bandages, triangular	4
Betadine brushes	24
Blanket, disposable emergency	2
Blood pressure cuff	1
Burnsheet	2

Dressings, multitrauma sterile	24
Eye irrigation kit	1
Eye patches	22
Food wrap plastic	2 boxes
Gloves, sterile	2 pair
Lubricant, water-soluble	1 tube
Ointment, antiseptic	4 tubes, 2 oz. ea.
Pads, compression	4
Pads, gauze	4" X 4", 1 box of 50
	8" x 8", 1 box of 50
Pads, petroleum gauze	1 box of 50
Shears, emergency	1 pair
Stethoscope	1
Tape, waterproof	2", 100'
	4", 100'
Tongue depressors	1 box of 100
Tourniquets	2

Airway, Breathing, Circulation Supplies:

Airway Kit:

*Oxygen	1 D cylinder with integral pressure regulator and tubing
Bag-valve-mask device	1
Pocket mask w/oxygen inlet	1
Oxygen mask	1
Oxygen cannula	1
Oxygen tubing	2 sets
Portable suction unit and tubing	1
Oral airways	1 set with 7 sizes
McGill forceps	1 pair

---

*Oxygen, one of the most effective substances available for sustaining life in a trauma situation, legally is a drug and must be prescribed by a physician. One E cylinder containing 22 cubic feet of oxygen at 2,000 psi will provide a typical 5 liter/min. flow for approximately two hours. With a regulator to reduce its pressure to 50 psi, it will weigh approximately 12 pounds. (To compute the usage rate in minutes of an oxygen cylinder: multiply its capacity in cubic feet by 28.32 [liters/cubic feet], subtract 50 to account for

Fracture-, Neck-, and Spinal-Injury Supplies:

Ladder or air splints	1 kit of assorted types and sizes
Cervical collars	1 kit with 3 sizes
Sandbags	2 of 3 pounds ea.
Long spine-board or scoop stretcher	1

Severe Bleeding/Circulation Supplies:

Scissors, surgical	1 pair
Steri-strips	2 boxes in assorted sizes
Suture kit, 4/0 nylon and needles	4 kits
Curved forceps	1 pair
Hemostats	2 pair
Xylocaine, topical	2 aerosol cans
Military Antishock Trousers (MAST)	1 pair

Body-Fluid Replacement Supplies:

Arm board	1
Large-bore IV catheter with large-bore tubing	4 sets in various sizes

MEDICATIONS KIT

Item	Quantity
Codeine	
Oral	50 caps, 30 mg. ea.
Injectable	10 prefilled syringes, 60 mg. ea.

pressure-regulator consumption, then divide the result by the liters per minute of flow.) Oxygen must be stored away from excess heat and clearly marked with a warning sign prohibiting smoking, open flames, or electrical sparks.

Note: Never use medications past their expiration date as their chemical composition may have altered.

For further reading on emergency medical procedures and supplies, see *Basic Trauma Life Support*, 2nd edition, John E. Campbell et al., Prentice-Hall, 1988.

Demerol
    Oral   50 caps, 25 mg. ea.
    Injectable   10 prefilled syringes, 100 mg. ea.
Dextrose, 50% solution   6 bags, 1000cc ea.
Epinephrine (1:1000 type)
    Injectable   10 prefilled syringes, 0.5 mg. ea.
Morphine
    Injectable   10 prefilled syringes, 10 mg. ea.
Narcan (IV push)   4 prefilled syringes, 0.4 mg. ea.
Nitroglycerine   50 tablets, 0.4 mg. ea.
Oxygen   12 E cylinders, 22 cu. ft. ea.
Penicillin
    Oral   50 caps., 500 mg. ea.
    Injectable   10 prefilled syringes, 1.2
                                          million units ea.
Plasmanate   6 bags, 250cc ea.
Ringerslactate   6 bags, 1000cc ea.
Tetanus toxoid   5 prefilled syringes, 0.5 mg. ea.

Spare Parts and Supplies

As you assemble your spare-parts inventory for either coastal or offshore cruising, here is a list of replacement items and supplies you should at least consider having on board:

Engine

Alternator or generator
Drive belts
Starter motor
Starter switch
Starter solenoid
Raw-water pump
Fuel pump
Thermostat and gasket
Injectors
Valve cover gasket
Mechanical gauges and sensors:
    RPM
    Coolant temperature
    Oil Pressure

Fuel Filters
    Primary
    Secondary
Fuel biocide
Oil
Oil filters
Fuel-line hose and fittings
Oil-line hose and fittings

Transmission

Oil or fluid
Mechanical drive oil-
    temperature gauge

Underwater Gear

Shaft
Strut and bearings
Propeller
Rudder
Appropriate nuts, bolts,
    washers, shaft keys,
    lubricants, and sealants
Shaft zincs
Rudder zincs

Hydraulic System

Hydraulic line and fittings
Hydraulic valve
Hydraulic pump
Hydraulic fluid

AC Electrical System

Generator relay
Generator circuit board
Generator starter switch
Generator starter solenoid
Circuit breakers
    120 volt of appropriate
        amperage ratings
    240 volt of appropriate
        amperage ratings
Air conditioning/heating
    unit relay
Refrigeration compressor
    relay
Incandescent light bulbs
Fluorescent light tubes
120-volt light switch
120-volt receptacle

DC Electrical System

Circuit breakers of appro-
    priate amperage ratings

Fuses appropriate to all
    onboard DC equipment
Electronic compass sensor
Light switch
Pump switch
Marine head switch
Windlass switch
Depth-sounder transducer

Water/Waste System

Marine-head seal kits
Marine-head supply pump
Marine-head macerator
    pump
Watermaker supply pump
Bilge pump
Water pump
Impellers appropriate to all
    onboard water pumps
Water heater element

Water hoses, fittings, and
    clamps
Water pipes and fittings
Water purification tablets
Assorted plumbing washers

Tender/Outboard

Outboard spark plug
Outboard ignition kit
Coil
Condenser
Outboard motor oil
Outboard fuel supply line
Steering cable, clamps, and
    pulleys

INDEX

Numerals in *italics* indicate illustrations

215

helicopter evacuation, 65-73; from life raft, 29-30; guiding litter to deck, 66, 70, 71, *71*; hoisting litter, 66, 72-73; how to request, 65, 67; preparations for, 65, 68-70; when to request, 65, 67, 115, 121-22, 125, 127, 135, 138, 141, 144-46

helicopters, air-sea search and rescue, 28, 29-30

High Sea Stations, 186; channels and frequencies listed, 184-86

hose, raw-water intake, 77

hull, protecting while grounded, 50

hull damage, 75-81; causes of, 76; checking for source, 76; distress signals, 75, 80-81; in grounding, 46; pumping water, 79-80; stemming water flow, 77-78, *78*, 79

hull insurance, 56

hydraulic systems trouble: diesel-engine governor, 166; steering, 169; supplies and parts list, 217; transmission, 168

hypothermia, 13, 23, 26, 140-41, 145

I

ignition switch, engine, *154*, 155, 156, 158, 159, 161; checking, 157

ignition system, gasoline engine, *154*, 161-64

immersion suits, 11, 12, 13

impeller, engine cooling-system pump, 160

injector pump, diesel engi. *155*, 159, 165, 167

inlet, running, in adverse conditions, 57, 58-59

insect bites or stings, 128, 132

insulin shock, 102, 133-35; causes of, 133, 134; symptoms of, 102, 133, 134, 135; treatment of, 134

insurance, towing coverage, 55, 56

internal bleeding, 102, 114-15, 145

International Distress, Safety, and Calling Channels: SSB, 183; VHF, 182

international ship-to-ship radio channels, 16, 182, 183

intership safety radio channels, 182, 183

ITU Channels, 16, 183-86; frequency list, 184-86; planned changeover 183 *n.*

J-K

jack lines, in heavy weather, 57, 58

jellyfish stings, 128-29

jury rig, 153, 168-69; of rudder, 170

kedge anchor, use to extract from grounding, 48, 49, *49*, 50

kedging off, to extract from grounding, 49

L

land, swimming for, 22-23

leaks, 75-80; *see also* hull damage

Lewis, Richard J., 127-28

lieing a-hull, sailboat, 64

life jackets, 11, 12-13, 31, 35, 57, 58, 86, 90; type needed, 13

life raft, 18-22, 31, 35; inflating, 13, 18; lashing to vessel, 18; launching, 11, 18, *19*; loading, 19; rationing water and provisions, 25-26; signaling from, 20-21, 23-25, 28, 29; survival supply drop to, 30; survival tips, 22-27; tethering to vessel, 11, 13, 18, 21-22

life ring, for MOB, 86, 90

lubrication system, engine, 155, 159

lung puncture wounds, 117-18, 145

M

"Man Overboard" (MOB) 83-98; approaching, tips for, 90-91, *91*, 92; hoisting aboard, 84, 90, 93-95; observing incident on another vessel, 190; Pan-Pan distress signal, 84, 93, 95-96, 98, 181, 187, 190; plotting the course to, 86-87, 96-98; powerboat maneuvers, 87-88, 93-94; radio-telephone alarm signal, 95, 187, 190; sailboat maneuvers, 88-90, *91*, 91-92; tips on conducting search, 96-98

marine animal poisoning, 128-29, 130, 132; emergency treatments, 130; possible complications, 130

mast, loss of, 168-69

Mayday distress call and message, 175,

N-O

P